Contents

OFFICE 2000

in easy steps

Stephen Copestake

In easy steps is an imprint of Computer Step
Southfield Road . Southam
Warwickshire CV33 OFB . England

Tel: 01926 817999 Fax: 01926 817005
http://www.computerstep.com

Notice of Liability

Every effort has been made to ensure that this book contains accurate
and current information. However, Computer Step and the author shall
not be liable for any loss or damage suffered by readers as a result of
any information contained herein.

Trademarks

Microsoft, Windows and Office 2000 are registered trademarks of
Microsoft Corporation. All other trademarks are acknowledged as
belonging to their respective companies.

Printed and bound in the United Kingdom

ISBN 1-84078-031-2

3 Excel 2000   105

A Common Approach

This chapter shows you how to get started quickly in any Office 2000 module. You'll learn to create new documents and open/save existing ones. You'll use the Shortcut bar to save time and energy, and also get information you need from on-line HELP and the Office Assistant. Finally, you'll edit files from Internet Explorer, and enhance your use of Office with additional features.

Chapter One

Covers

Introduction

 All editions of Office 2000 also include Internet Explorer 5 (IE5), Microsoft's Web browser. For more on this, see 'Internet Explorer 5' in this same series.

The Standard edition of Microsoft Office 2000 consists of four modules:

- Word 2000 – word-processor

- Excel 2000 – spreadsheet

- PowerPoint 2000 – presentation/slide show creator

- Outlook 2000 – personal/business information manager

Three at least of these programs are leaders in their respective fields. The point about Office, however, is that it integrates the four modules exceptionally well. With the exception of Outlook, which has to adopt a relatively individualistic approach, the modules share a common look and feel.

 Other editions of Office 2000 are as follows, with the modules they consist of:

- Small Business – Word, Excel, Outlook, Publisher

- Professional – Small Business+Standard+ Access

- Premium – Professional +PhotoDraw +FrontPage

- Developer – Premium +Developer tools

(Each of the above editions also comes with Small Business Tools.)

The illustration below shows the Word opening screen. Flagged are components which are common to PowerPoint, Outlook and Excel, too. (There are also, of course, differences between the module screens: Outlook, for instance, because of its very different nature, has fewer toolbars. We'll explore this in later chapters.)

Title bar   Menu bar

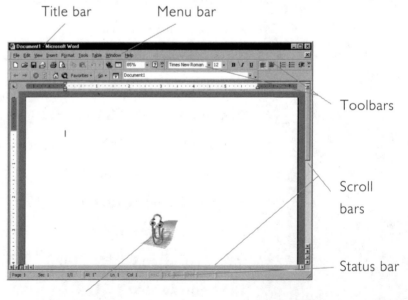

Toolbars

Scroll bars

Status bar

Office Assistant (for more on this, see pages 28–30)

Toolbars

Toolbars are important components in all four Office 2000 modules. A toolbar is an on-screen bar which contains shortcut buttons. These symbolise and allow easy access to often-used commands which would normally have to be invoked via one or more menus.

For example, Word 2000's Standard toolbar lets you:

- create, open, save and print documents

- perform copy & paste and cut & paste operations

- undo editing actions

- access Word's HELP system

by simply clicking on the relevant button.

Toolbars vary to some extent from module to module. We'll be looking at these in more detail as we encounter them. For the moment, some general advice.

Specifying which toolbars are displayed

In any Office module, pull down the View menu and click Toolbars. Now do the following:

To add a new button to a toolbar, right-click over the toolbar. Click Customize. In the dialog which launches, click the Commands tab. In the Categories field, click a category (a group of associated icons). In the Commands box, drag a button onto the toolbar *in the open document.* Finally, click Close.

This is Excel's toolbar list. Available toolbars in the other Office 2000 programs vary slightly.

✓	Standard
✓	Formatting
	Chart
	Clipboard
	Control Toolbox
✓	Drawing
	External Data
	Forms
	Picture
	PivotTable
	Reviewing
	Visual Basic
	Web
	WordArt
	Customize...

Click the toolbar you want to be visible – a ✔ appears against it

Repeat this procedure for as many toolbars as necessary.

Automatic customisation

Office 2000 menus expand automatically. Simply pull down the required menu, (which will at first be abbreviated) then wait a few seconds: it expands to display the full menu.

However, to expand them manually, click here on the chevrons at the bottom of the menu:

A long-standing anomaly in the use of software has been that, although different users use different features, no allowance has been made for this: the same features display on everyone's menus and toolbars...

Now this has changed. In the modules in Office 2000, menus and toolbars are now personalised.

Personalised menus

When you first use a module, its menus display the features which Microsoft believes are used 95% of the time. Features which are infrequently used are not immediately visible. This is made clear in the illustrations below:

Word 2000's Format menu, as it first appears...

As you use the Office 2000 modules, individual features are dynamically promoted or demoted in the relevant menus.

This means menus are continually evolving...

The expanded menu – the little-used features are shown in paler grey

Personalised toolbars

Toolbars in Office 2000 work on a similar principle to menus:

- if possible, they display on a single row

- they overlap when there isn't enough room on-screen

- icons are 'promoted' and 'demoted' like menu entries

Look at the illustration below:

Click here

 You can use this fly-out as an alternative way to add buttons to toolbars.
   Place the mouse pointer over Add or Remove Buttons. In the menu which appears, do one of the following:

- click an entry which doesn't have ☑ against it to add it to the toolbar

- click an entry which does have ☑ against it to remove it from the toolbar

Here, two of Word 2000's toolbars (Standard and Formatting) are displaying side by side. As a result, not all of the buttons display. Following step 1 above produces this result:

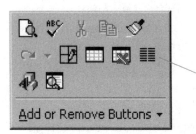

Icons Word has determined are little used display in a separate fly-out

To implement any of the hidden features, simply click the relevant icon.

Creating new documents

With the exception of Outlook (see Chapter 5), all Office 2000 modules let you:

- create new blank documents

- create new documents based on a 'template'

- create new documents with the help of a 'Wizard'

Because Word 2000, PowerPoint 2000 and Excel 2000 are uniform in the way they create new documents, we'll look at this topic here rather than in the later chapters, which are specific to each program.
(However, see Chapter 4 for specialised advice on creating new slide shows.)

Creating blank documents is the simplest route to new document creation; use this if you want to define the document components yourself from scratch. This is often not the most efficient or effective way to create new documents.

Templates – also known as boilerplates – are sample documents complete with the relevant formatting and/or text. By basing a new document on a template, you automatically have access to these.

Wizards are advanced templates which incorporate a question-and-answer system. You work through a series of dialogs, answering the appropriate questions and making the relevant choices.

Documents created with the use of templates or Wizards can easily be amended subsequently.

Both templates and Wizards are high-powered yet easy to use shortcuts to document creation. Office 2000 provides a large number of templates and Wizards. For example, Word offers Wizards which automate the production of newsletters, faxes, letters and memos, as well as numerous templates.

The topics that relate to the New dialog, templates and Wizards do not apply to Outlook.

All three document creation methods involve launching the New dialog. This can be accessed:

- by using the Office Shortcut bar

- from within the modified Windows Start menu

- from within the relevant Office 2000 program

Launching the New dialog

 See pages 31–35 for how to launch and work with the Shortcut bar.

Utilise any of the following methods:

A. Using the Shortcut bar

Within the Office Shortcut bar, do the following:

Click here

 If the Office toolbar isn't uppermost in the Shortcut bar, right-click on the bar. Click Office in the menu that appears.

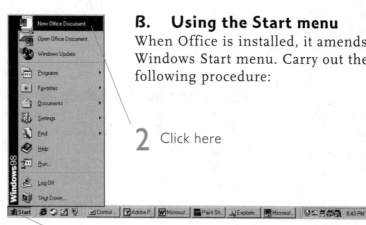

B. Using the Start menu

When Office is installed, it amends the Windows Start menu. Carry out the following procedure:

2 Click here

Click here

C. From within the program

In Word 2000, Excel 2000 or PowerPoint 2000, pull down the File menu and do the following:

The following keyboard shortcut is available in Word, PowerPoint and Excel. Simply press Ctrl+N.

Click here

Using the New dialog

The form the New dialog takes depends, to some extent, on which method you use to launch it. If you invoke it by using methods A or B on page 13, you get the full version which incorporates elements from Word, Excel and PowerPoint. You can then choose which type of new document you want to create.

If, on the other hand, you use method C on page 13, you get a specific, abbreviated form.

Using the full New dialog

First launch the New dialog (use technique A or B on page 13). Then do the following:

To create a blank document, activate the General tab and click the Blank Document (Word), Blank Workbook (Excel) or Blank Presentation (PowerPoint) icon.

The Preview section on the right provides an illustration of what your new document will look like (providing it's based on a template or Wizard).

Activate the relevant tab

New Office Document

Presentations | Publications | Reports | Spreadsheet ... | Web Pages | Office 97 T ... | Business Pl ...
General | Databases | Design Temp ... | Legal Pleadings | Letters & ... | Memos | Other Documents

Blank Document   Web Page   E-mail Message   Blank Workbook

Blank Presentation   AutoContent Wizard   Blank Database   Blank Publication

Preview

Preview not available.

OK   Cancel

2 Click the blank document, template or Wizard you want to use

3 Click here

In the above illustration, a new blank Word document is being created.

Using the program-specific New dialog

First launch the New dialog (method C on page 13) within the relevant Office 2000 module. Then do the following:

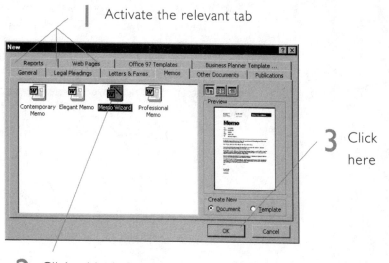

Activate the relevant tab

3 Click here

2 Click a blank document, template or Wizard

After step 3, further dialogs may launch – complete these by following the on-screen instructions.

In the above illustration, a new Word document is being created, based on the MEMO Wizard.

Notice that the only new document options you can access in this form of the New dialog are Word-specific.

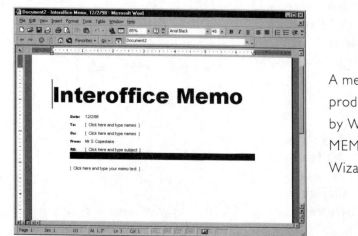

A memo produced by Word's MEMO Wizard

Working with templates

If you elected to base your new document on a template, Office 2000 creates a detailed document complete with preset text and formatting.

The illustration below shows a new PowerPoint 2000 slide show, based on the Marketing Plan template.

Outline

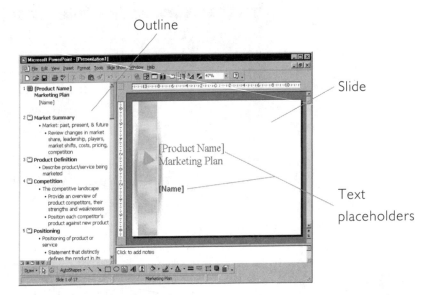

Slide

Text placeholders

See Chapter 4 for more information on how to use PowerPoint 2000.

This provides a good idea of how useful and sophisticated Office's templates are. In this case, Office 2000 has:

- created several slides (the first is currently showing) together with a textual outline

- inserted text placeholders (designed to be replaced, easily and conveniently, with your own text)

- applied a Design template, as appropriate

- applied a colour scheme, as appropriate

See page 20 for how to save Office 2000 documents.

- applied a layout style, as appropriate

- applied a background, as appropriate

Make the appropriate amendments, then save the template as a document in its own right.

Working with Wizards

When you elect to create a new document with the help of a Wizard, Office 2000 launches a succession of dialogs. The illustration below is the first dialog when you run the Word Fax Wizard.

Complete the dialog (if appropriate)

Then click here

 Office 2000 tells you when you've reached the final dialog by dimming the Next button.

Whichever Wizard you use, in whichever Office module, complete the necessary fields and/or click the necessary options. Then click Next to move on to the next dialog. Continue doing this until you reach the final dialog. Then do the following:

 See the 'Publishing to the Internet' topic (page 23) for how to use the Web Page Wizard in Word.

Click here

The end result of using a Wizard is the same as using a template: a feature-rich document which you can amend as necessary.

Opening Office 2000 documents

We saw earlier that Office 2000 lets you create new documents in various ways. You can also open Word 2000, Excel 2000 and PowerPoint 2000 documents you've already created.

For how to open an existing schedule or contact/task list in Outlook 2000, see Chapter 5.

In any module apart from Outlook, pull down the File menu and click Open. Now carry out steps 1–5 below, as appropriate:

3 Click here. In the drop-down list, click the relevant drive/folder combination

In Excel 2000, (providing you're using Internet Explorer 4.01 or higher) you can interact with Web-based spreadsheets you open using the procedures overleaf. For instance, you can:

- enter data;
- create formulas;
- recalculate and sort/ filter data, and;
- perform basic formatting,

directly from within the browser.

Open	? X
Look in:	Chap.01

17-4
New3.ppt

Recommending a Strategy

Ideas for Today and Tomorrow

File name:

Files of type: All PowerPoint Presentations (*.ppt;*.pps;*.pot;*.htm;*.h

4 Click the file

5 Click here

1 Make sure the correct file type (e.g. All PowerPoint Presentations) is shown. If it isn't, click the arrow and follow step 2

All Files (*.*)
All PowerPoint Presentations (*.ppt;*.pps;*.pot;*.htm;*.h
Presentations and Shows (*.ppt;*.pps)
Web Pages (*.htm; *.html)
Design Templates (*.pot)
Freelance Windows 1.0-2.1 (*.pre)

2 Click a file type

Opening Internet documents

In any of the Office modules (apart from Outlook), you can open documents stored at FTP sites on the World Wide Web or on Intranets.

If the Web toolbar isn't currently on-screen, move the mouse pointer over any existing toolbar and right-click. In the menu which appears, click Web. Now do the following:

To open Internet documents, you must have a live connection to the Internet. (For more information on Internet access and the Internet in general, see 'Internet UK in easy steps'.)

After step 4, the Web/ Intranet site selected in step 3 is opened in your browser.

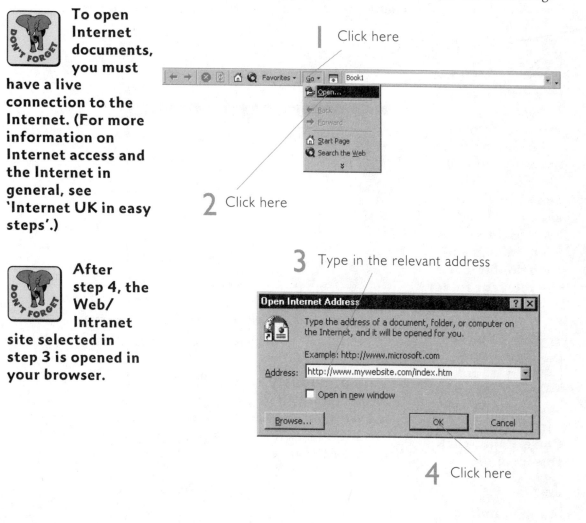

1 Click here

2 Click here

3 Type in the relevant address

4 Click here

Saving Office 2000 documents

It's important to save your work at frequent intervals, in order to avoid data loss in the event of a hardware fault or power interruption. With the exception of Outlook, Office 2000 uses a consistent approach to saving.

Saving a document for the first time

In Word, Excel or PowerPoint, pull down the File menu and click Save. Or press Ctrl+S. Now do the following:

Re step 2 – click any buttons here:

for access to the relevant folders.

(For instance, to save files to your Desktop, click Desktop. Or, to save files inside Web folders, click Web Folders and then double-click the relevant folder.)

2 Click here. In the drop-down list, click a drive/ folder combination

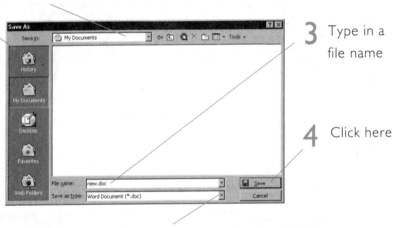

3 Type in a file name

4 Click here

Click here. In the list, click the format you want to save to

You can use a shortcut for either save method.

In Word, Excel or PowerPoint, click this icon:

in the Standard toolbar.

Saving previously saved documents

In Word, Excel or PowerPoint, pull down the File menu and click Save. Or press Ctrl+S. No dialog launches; instead, Office 2000 saves the latest version of your document to disk, overwriting the previous version.

Saving to the Internet

To publish your Office documents to the Web, you must have a live connection to the Internet. (For more information on Internet access and the Internet in general, see 'Internet UK in easy steps'.)

In any of the Office 2000 modules (apart from Outlook), you can save documents (usually in HTML – HyperText Markup Language – format) to:

- a pre-established Web folder (Web folders are shortcuts to Web servers)

- a pre-established FTP site on the World Wide Web

(See the HOT TIPS for how to set up Web folders/FTP sites.)

You can also save HTML files directly to Intranets, using the same techniques.

HTML enhancements

While Office 2000 modules preserve their own native formats (*.doc, *.xls and *.ppt) so that they're identical with the formats used by Office 97, the standard Web format (*.html or *.htm) has had the following changes made:

For how to set up a Web folder, see the HOT TIP on page 36.

- it's now a Companion File format (Microsoft regards it as occupying the same status as its proprietary formats); this means that you can create *and* share rich Web documents with the same Office 2000 tools used to create printed documents

- it now duplicates the functionality of the proprietary formats (i.e. all the usual Office 2000 features are preserved when saving in HTML format)

- you can edit HTML files from within Internet Explorer (see page 26)

To set up a FTP site, open the Save As dialog in any Office module. Click the 'Save in' field. In the list, select Add/ Modify FTP Locations. Complete the dialog, then click Add. Click OK, then press Esc.

- it's now recognised by the Windows Clipboard. This means that data can be copied from Internet Explorer and pasted directly into an application such as Word 2000

- from within Office 2000 programs, you can preview your work directly in Internet Explorer, before you've saved your work to disk (see page 22)

...cont'd

To close your browser, press Alt+F4.

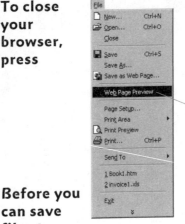

Before you can save files to Web folders or FTP sites, you must first have carried out the relevant procedures in the two HOT TIPS on page 21.

Previewing your work before saving

In any module apart from Outlook, pull down the File menu and do the following:

Click here

Office 2000 now launches your browser, with your work displayed in it.

Saving your work to a Web folder or FTP site

In any module apart from Outlook, pull down the File menu and click Save as Web Page. Then do the following:

Click here. In the drop-down list, select a recipient – see the HOT TIP

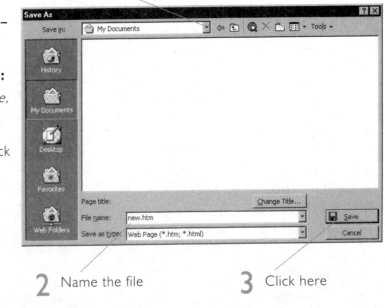

Re step 1 – do one of the following:

• *To save to a FTP site*, click FTP Locations. Double-click a FTP site, then double-click where you want to save to

• *To save to a Web server*, click Web Folders. Activate a Web folder

2 Name the file

3 Click here

Publishing to the Internet

On pages 21–22, we discussed how to convert existing Office 2000 documents into HTML format and – at the same time – save them on the Web or to Intranets. However, in Word 2000 you can also use another method. You can run the Web Page Wizard to create a *new* Web document from scratch and then copy the relevant HTML files to an Internet or Intranet site (see the DON'T FORGET icon on the left).

 You can use Windows Explorer to publish your completed Word documents on the Web – see the DON'T FORGET tips and HOT TIP on pages 36–37.
   Alternatively, you can open the new Web files, then use the relevant procedures on page 22 to save them to the appropriate FTP site.

In Word 2000, pull down the File menu and click New. Now do the following:

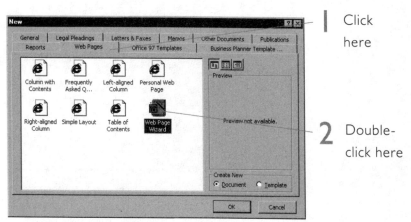

1 Click here

2 Double-click here

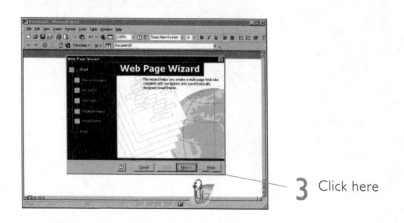

3 Click here

Now complete the additional steps on pages 24–25.

Re step 4 – enter a name and site address for your new Web document.

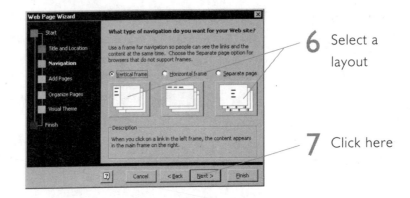

4 Complete these fields

5 Click here

6 Select a layout

7 Click here

 Re step 8 – if you select Add Template Page or Add Existing File, complete the additional dialog which launches. Then carry out step 9.

8 Optional – to add a new component, click one or more buttons

9 Click here

...cont'd

Re step 10 – to adjust the page sequence, select the page you want to move. Now click Move Up or Move Down.
   Repeat as often as necessary.

Re steps 12–15 – these add a theme (a preset formatting scheme) to your Web site.

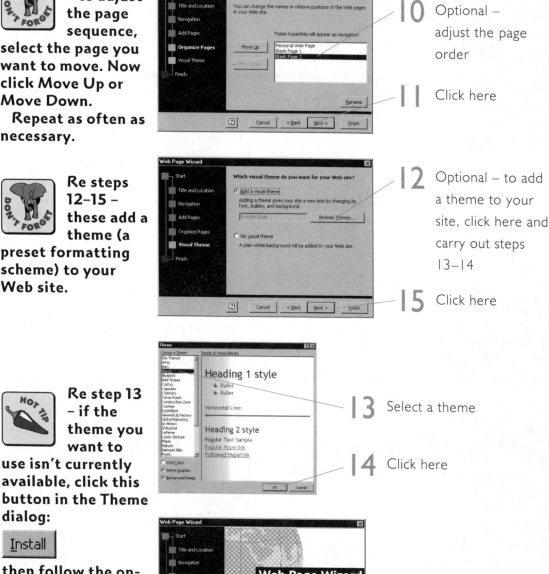

10   Optional – adjust the page order

11   Click here

12   Optional – to add a theme to your site, click here and carry out steps 13–14

15   Click here

13   Select a theme

14   Click here

HOT TIP

Re step 13 – if the theme you want to use isn't currently available, click this button in the Theme dialog:

`Install`

then follow the on-screen instructions.
   (This is Office 2000's Install on Demand feature in operation.)

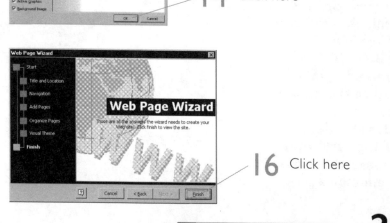

16   Click here

Editing in Internet Explorer

Using the technique discussed here,
Office 2000 files, converted to HTML format and saved to the Web can be run by the majority of Internet users.

When you create HTML files from within Office 2000 modules (see below), they can be edited from within Internet Explorer 5.

Look at the illustration below:

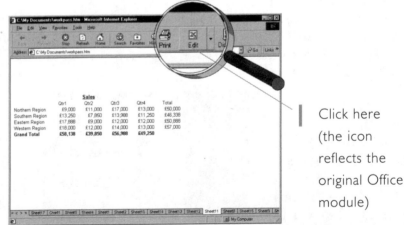

See pages 171–172 for how to run slide shows in Internet Explorer 5 itself.

This is a simple Excel 2000 worksheet. You can use the techniques discussed on page 20 to convert it to a HTML file – in step 1, however, choose Web Page (*.htm; *.html). Once the HTML file has been opened in Internet Explorer, do the following:

After step 1, the file is opened within the originating Office 2000 module, with the formatting intact despite the 'round-trip'.
  Use standard editing techniques to make the relevant amendments.

Click here
(the icon
reflects the
original Office
module)

Using Office's HELP system

Office supports the standard Windows HELP system. For instance:

Office calls these highly specific HELP bubbles 'ToolTips'. ToolTips are a specialised form of ScreenTips (see below).

- Moving the mouse pointer over toolbar buttons produces an explanatory HELP bubble:

- You can move the mouse pointer over fields in dialogs, commands or screen areas and produce a specific HELP box. Carry out the following procedure to achieve this:

Office calls these highly specific HELP topics 'ScreenTips'.

Right-clicking a field and left-clicking the box which launches...

Displays Help text, explaining what the command does.

...produces a specific HELP topic

Other standard Windows HELP features are also present; see your Windows documentation for how to use these. Additionally, all the Office 2000 applications have inbuilt HELP in the normal way...

Office 2000 also has one unique HELP feature: the Office Assistant. See the next topic.

The Office Assistant

Office 2000 has a unique HELP feature which is designed to make it much easier to become productive: the Office Assistant. The Assistant:

To close an Office Assistant window at any time, press Esc, or click the Close button.

- answers questions directly. This is an especially useful feature for the reason that, normally when you invoke a program's HELP system, you know more or less the question you want to ask, or the topic on which you need information. If neither of these is true, however, the Office Assistant responds to plain English questions and provides a choice of answers. For example, responses produced by entering 'What are ToolTips?' include:

  — *Show or hide shortcut keys in ToolTips*

  — *Show or hide toolbar ScreenTips*

  — *Rename a menu command or toolbar button*

The Office Assistant is animated. It can also change shape! To do this, click the Options button. In the dialog which appears, activate the Gallery tab. Click the Next button until the Assistant you want is displayed. Click OK, then follow any further on-screen instructions.

- offers HELP which relates to the module being used

- provides context-sensitive tips

- answers questions entered in your own words

What would you like to do?

- Using macros to automate tasks
- Create a macro

What are tooltips?

Options   Search

The Word 2000 Office Assistant, after it has just launched

If the HELP bubble isn't displayed, simply click anywhere in the Assistant:

...cont'd

Every so often, the Assistant displays a useful tip. To view it, do the following:

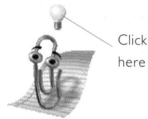

Click here

When you've finished with it, do this:

Click here

If you don't want to use the Office Assistant at all, do the following. Click here: In the Office Assistant dialog, activate the Options tab. Deselect Use the Office Assistant. Click OK.

Launching the Office Assistant
By default, the Office Assistant displays automatically. If it isn't currently on-screen, however, refer to the Standard toolbar and do the following:

Click here

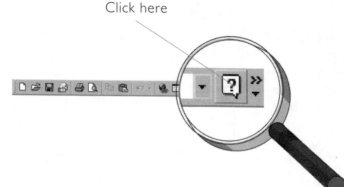

Hiding the Office Assistant
If you don't want the Office Assistant to display, right-click over it and do the following:

Click here

Unhiding the Office Assistant
To display the Assistant after you've hidden it, pull down the Help menu and click Show the Office Assistant.

...cont'd

If the Assistant doesn't provide the right answer, you can send your query to a special Web site with more information.
Ensure your Internet connection is live, then do the following:

You can use the Office Assistant (whatever its current incarnation) to ask questions in plain English. The advantage of using the Assistant to do this is that you can use it to find information on topics which you aren't sure how to classify.

Asking questions

First, ensure the Office Assistant is visible. Then do the following:

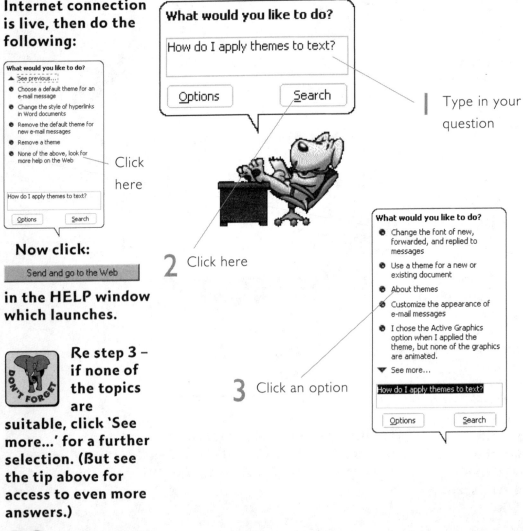

Now click:

Send and go to the Web

in the HELP window which launches.

Re step 3 – if none of the topics are suitable, click 'See more...' for a further selection. (But see the tip above for access to even more answers.)

The Shortcut bar – an overview

Windows 98/2000 is an exception to this, in that you _can_ create program buttons in the Quick Launch section of the Taskbar:

A button to start Word 2000 has been added...

However, the Shortcut bar is easier to use, and more convenient.

If the Shortcut bar isn't currently on-screen, do the following.

Click the Windows Start button. Then click Programs, Microsoft Office Tools, Microsoft Office Shortcut Bar.

The main function of the Windows Taskbar is to switch between already open applications. However, it doesn't let you start programs directly with a single click on a button (instead, you have to use the normal Start menu route, which requires several clicks and/or mouse movements). The Office Shortcut bar rectifies this omission. You can add buttons for any programs you want, and start them very quickly and easily.

The Shortcut bar also mimics the Taskbar, but with one important difference. If a program is already open, clicking on its button on the Shortcut bar switches to it and also opens a new blank window. (This only works with Office 2000 programs; if you try it with other applications, a second copy launches instead.)

You can determine the Shortcut bar's on-screen location. Additionally, you can have it display permanently, or 'auto-hide' it (where it only appears on screen when you move the mouse pointer to a specific screen area).

Toolbars

Buttons on the Shortcut bar are organised into specialist _toolbars_. The main ones are:

Office	has buttons relating specifically to Office 2000 modules
Programs	has buttons representing program folders
Desktop	has buttons representing items on your Desktop (e.g. My Computer, Internet Explorer and Recycle Bin)
Accessories	has buttons representing programs normally accessed from the Start/Accessories menu (e.g. Notepad, WordPad and Paint)
Favorites	has links to Web (and other) sites you've designated as Favorites

You can display as many, or as few, toolbars as you want.

Displaying Shortcut bar toolbars

Only four of the available toolbars are currently displaying (Accessories is hidden) – see 'Hiding/revealing toolbars' below for how to remedy this.

Office uses a unique effect when you have more than one toolbar displayed at once on the Shortcut bar: it *layers* them.

Look at the illustration below:

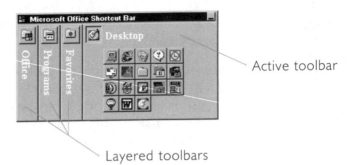

Active toolbar

Layered toolbars

Here, the Shortcut bar is 'floating'; for how to display it on the top, bottom, left or right of your screen instead, see page 33.

To make another toolbar active, simply left-click on it.

Hiding/revealing toolbars

To display a toolbar, move the mouse pointer over the Shortcut bar and right-click once. Now do the following:

To hide a toolbar, click its entry – the tick disappears.

Click any toolbar to select it – a ✔ appears against its entry

Re the tips on the facing page – you may have to buy further Office 2000 Proofing Tools if you want to work in languages other than Spanish and French.

Repeat this procedure for however many toolbars you want to hide or reveal.

Specifying the Shortcut bar location

The Office 2000 modules each come with a single program file which:

- has a global interface (you can switch languages seamlessly)

- (in the case of Word 2000) lets you use AutoCorrect in multiple languages

- (in the case of Word 2000) provides a worldwide Thesaurus – the result should be an increase in available proofing tools

To turn on multiple language editing, click the Windows Start button. Select Programs, Microsoft Office Tools, Microsoft Office Language Settings. In the dialog, select an installed Office version, then the new language(s) you want to use. Click OK.

You can have the Shortcut bar display on the left or right, or on the top or bottom of your screen. Alternatively, you can have it 'float' on screen, as a separate window. Use whichever method is most convenient for the task in hand.

Positioning the Shortcut bar on the screen edge

To move the Shortcut bar to the top, bottom, left or right of your screen (Office calls this 'docking'), place the mouse pointer anywhere over the Shortcut bar (but not over one of the buttons). Hold down the left mouse button and drag the bar to the appropriate area. When you release the button, the bar 'docks' automatically.

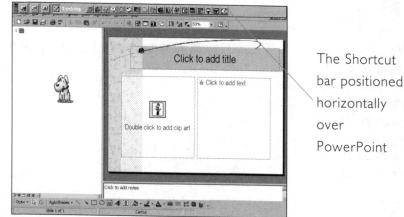

The Shortcut bar positioned horizontally over PowerPoint

Restoring the Shortcut bar to its previous location

Double-click the title bar:

Title bar   Shortcut buttons

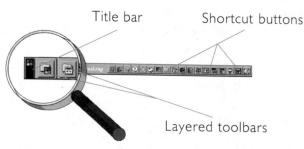

Layered toolbars

Auto-hiding the Shortcut bar

For more information on how to interact with the Shortcut bar when it's floating, see your Windows documentation.

You can also use a shortcut to Auto-Hide the Shortcut bar. Right-click over the bar; in the menu which appears, click Auto Hide. (This procedure also revokes Auto-Hide, if required.)

If the Shortcut bar is floating (not docked), Auto-Hide has no immediate effect on it.

When it's floating, the Shortcut bar behaves much like any other window. For example, if it's minimised, clicking on the Shortcut bar button on the Taskbar:

> Microsoft Of...

maximises it.

If it's docked, on the other hand, the Shortcut bar can be made to conceal itself bashfully when not required (this is called Auto-Hide). To do this, double-click in the Shortcut bar (but *not* on a button, or in the Title bar). Now do the following:

Ensure the View tab is active

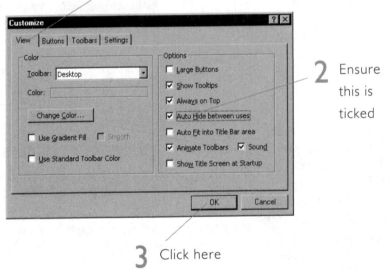

2 Ensure this is ticked

3 Click here

Making the Shortcut bar reappear temporarily

To make the Shortcut bar visible again when you need it, simply move the mouse pointer to the edge of the screen where the Office Shortcut bar is docked. For instance, if the bar was docked on the bottom of the screen, move the pointer as far down as it will go.

When you've finished, move the mouse pointer away from the docking area; the Shortcut bar disappears again.

Adding buttons to the Shortcut bar

You can add buttons that represent files to the Shortcut bar. These files can be program files, or just about any other kind of file.

Double-click in the Shortcut bar (but *not* on a button, or in the Title bar). Now do the following:

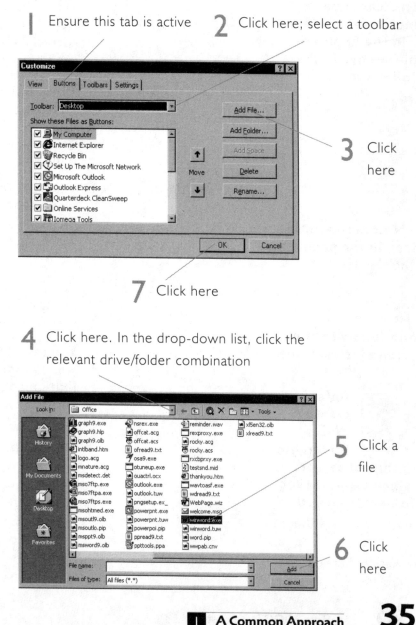

1 Ensure this tab is active

2 Click here; select a toolbar

3 Click here

7 Click here

4 Click here. In the drop-down list, click the relevant drive/folder combination

5 Click a file

6 Click here

Additional features – an overview

The first step in using Windows Explorer to work with Web servers is to create one or more Web folders.

In the Explorer hierarchy, do the following:

Click here

Now activate this icon in the pane on the right:

Add Web Folder

and follow the on-screen instructions.

Before you create a Web folder, get details of servers which support Web folders from your:

- system administrator, or:
- Internet Service Provider

Office 2000 provides the following extra features which are designed to enhance and/or speed up the way you work:

Quick File Switching

This allows you to switch to open documents within Office 2000 programs more easily and conveniently

Problem correction

Office 2000 identifies and corrects a wide variety of problems

Install on Demand

You can install only those features you want to use at the moment – other features can easily be installed later, when required

Collect and Paste

You can now copy and store as many as 12 items of text and/or pictures, and then paste them into Office 2000 documents at will

Web file management

You can use Windows Explorer to copy files to some Web servers – see the HOT TIP

Web discussions

You can embed conversations and comments in documents (but only on servers running Office Server Extensions)

Document subscription

You can 'subscribe' to documents (but only on servers running Office Server Extensions) and be notified of changes (file revisions, deletions, new files, etc.) automatically

Quick File Switching

To use Quick File Switching you need:

- Windows 98/2000, or:
- Windows 95 with Internet Explorer 4.0 (or a later version).

Once you've created one or more Web folders (see the tips on page 36), you can use Windows Explorer to copy files to them in the normal way.

This is one way to publish your Office 2000 documents to Internet or Intranet sites – see pages 21–22 for more information.

In the past, only programs (not individual windows within programs) displayed on the Windows Taskbar. With Office 2000, however, all open windows display as separate buttons.

In the following example, four new documents have been created in Word 2000. All four display as separate windows, although only one copy of Word 2000 is running:

Four Word 2000 windows

This is clarified by a glance at Word 2000's Window menu which (as before) shows all open Word windows:

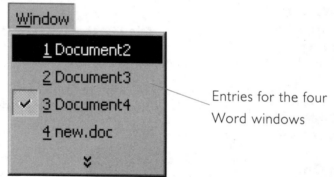

Entries for the four Word windows

Use this technique to go to a document window by simply clicking its Taskbar button, a considerable saving in time and effort.

Repairing errors

If Office Server Extensions have been installed on a Web server, you can add discussions to Office documents (inc. HTML files) stored on it.

In any Office program apart from Outlook, open a document. Ensure your Internet connection is live. Pull down the Tools menu and click Online Collaboration, Web Discussions. The Discussion Options dialog appears. (If it doesn't, click the Discussions button in the toolbar at the base of the screen and select Discussion Options in the menu.)

Click Add. Complete the Add or Edit Discussion Servers dialog. Click OK twice.

Office 2000 provides the following:

Automatic repair

Whenever you launch an Office 2000 application, it:

1. determines if essential files are missing or corrupted

2. automatically reinstalls the files

3. repairs incorrect entries (relating to missing or corrupted files) in the Windows Registry

Manual repair

There are other potential problems which, though far less serious, can still result in lost productivity – e.g. corrupted fonts and missing templates.

Office 2000 applications have a special diagnostic procedure (called 'Detect and Repair') which you can run when necessary. The procedure:

1. scrutinises the original state of your installation

2. compares this with the present state of your installation

3. takes the appropriate remedial steps

To run Detect and Repair in any Office 2000 module, pull down the Help menu and do the following:

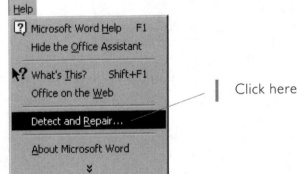

Click here

Office 2000 now detects and remedies any problem – this process may take some time.

Install on Demand

To subscribe to a document on a server running Office Server Extensions, first open it. Pull down the Tools menu and click Online Collaboration, Web Discussions. (If necessary, select a discussion server in the Discussion Options dialog and click OK.) In the Discussions toolbar, click the Subscribe button.
   Now follow the on-screen instructions.

To add a theme to a Word file, click Theme in the Format menu. Carry out step 1 (and 2, if required). Click OK.

Networked users may be asked to refer to a specific server location instead...

The Office 2000 applications make use of a new feature which allows users to install programs and program components on demand, only when they're needed. The following display within the host programs:

* shortcuts

* icons

* menu entries

for the uninstalled features.

An example of Install on Demand is themes. By default, only a few themes are copied to the user's hard disk. When you attempt to apply a theme which hasn't been installed, you're invited to rectify this. Do the following:

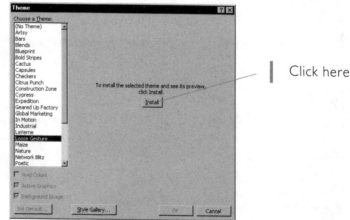

Click here

After a pause, step 1 typically produces a further dialog. Insert the original Office 2000 CD and carry out step 2:

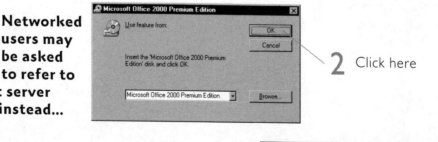

2 Click here

Collect and Paste

Until Office 2000, if you wanted to copy-and-paste multiple items of text and/or pictures into a document, it was necessary (since the Windows Clipboard can only hold one item at a time) to perform each operation separately. Now, however, you can use the new Collect and Paste operation to make this much easier.

Using Collect and Paste

From within Word, Excel, PowerPoint or Outlook, use standard procedures to copy multiple examples of text and/ or pictures – after the first copy, the Clipboard Toolbar launches. Do the following:

1 Copy each of the four words, and then copy the picture

The Clipboard Toolbar – in the top row, all four words have been copied, while the bottom row shows the copied picture

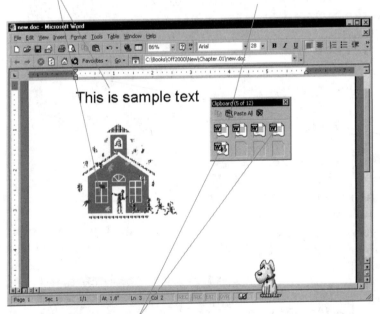

2 Click where you want to paste the item in your document, then click on an icon to paste in the contents. Or, click the Paste All button to paste in the whole Clipboard contents

Word 2000

Chapter Two

This chapter gives you the fundamentals of using Word 2000. You'll learn how to enter text, send e-mail and work with the Word screen. You'll also format text and create/apply text styles. Finally, you'll proof your documents, create summaries, bookmarks and hyperlinks, insert pictures and then customise page layout and printing.

Covers

The Word 2000 screen

Below is a detailed illustration of the Word 2000 screen.

 This is an incarnation of the Office Assistant (for more on this, see Chapter 1).

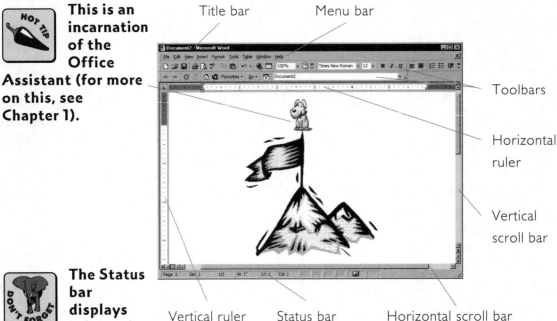

Title bar

Menu bar

Toolbars

Horizontal ruler

Vertical scroll bar

Vertical ruler

Status bar

Horizontal scroll bar

The Status bar displays information relating to the active document (e.g. what page you're on).

Some of these – e.g. the rulers and scroll bars – are standard to just about all programs that run under Windows. Many of them can be hidden, if required.

Specifying which screen components display

Pull down the Tools menu and click Options. Then:

1 Ensure the View tab is active

2 Click components in the Show section to select/ deselect them

3 Click here

Entering text

You can also use Click and Type to enter text almost anywhere in a document, without inserting the necessary paragraph marks or formatting – see pages 44–45.

Word 2000 lets you enter text immediately after you've started it (you can do this because a new blank document is automatically created based on the default template). In Word, you enter text at the insertion point:

A magnified view of the Word text insertion point

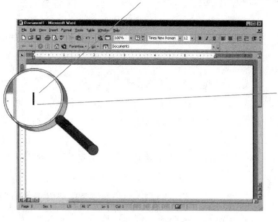

Begin entering text here

You can have Word insert words/ phrases for you.

Place the insertion point where you want the text inserted. Pull down the Insert menu and click AutoText. In the sub-menu, click a category (e.g. Salutation) then a glossary entry (e.g. Dear Sir or Madam); Word inserts the entry.

Additional characters

Most of the text you need to enter can be typed in directly from the keyboard. However, it's sometimes necessary to enter special characters, e.g. bullets (for instance: ✍) or special symbols like ©.

Pull down the Insert menu and click Symbol. Now do the following:

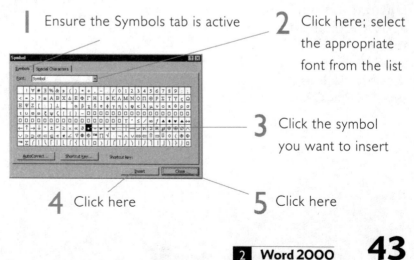

1 Ensure the Symbols tab is active

2 Click here; select the appropriate font from the list

3 Click the symbol you want to insert

4 Click here

5 Click here

Click and Type

You can also enter text in a special way in Word 2000, one that makes the process much easier. With Click and Type:

- you can enter text or pictures in most blank page areas, with the minimum of mouse activity

- you don't have to apply the necessary formatting yourself – Word 2000 does this automatically (e.g. you can insert text to the right of an existing paragraph without having to insert manual tab stops)

Using Click and Type

Ensure you're using Web Layout or Print Layout view. Position the mouse pointer where you want to insert text or a picture. Click once – the pointer changes to indicate the formatting which Word 2000 will apply:

 You can't use Click and Type in these blank page areas:

- bulleted lists
- numbered lists
- to the left and right of *indented* paragraphs
- to the left and right of pictures which have had top or bottom text wrap applied

 If Click and Type isn't enabled, pull down the Tools menu and click Options. In the Options dialog, activate the Edit tab. In the Click and type section, select 'Enable click and type'. Click OK.

Here, the pointer shows that Word 2000 is about to centre new text...

Now double-click, then do the following:

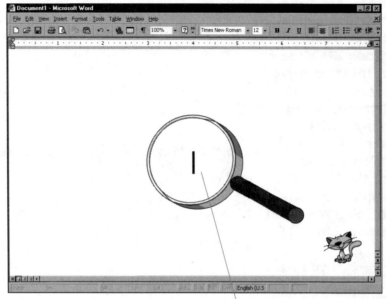

 If you use Click and Type beneath an existing text paragraph, Word 2000 applies a specific style to the new text. You can specify the style used.

Pull down the Tools menu and click Options. In the Options dialog, activate the Edit tab. In the Click and type section, click in this field:

In the drop-down list, select a style. Finally, click OK.

Begin entering text, or insert a picture in the normal way

The Click and Type pointers

The main pointers are:

Left-align

Centre-align

Right-align

Left-indent

Sending e-mail

To send e-mail from Word, you must have specified Outlook 2000 as your Internet e-mail program.
   Within Internet Explorer, click Internet Options in the Tools menu. Click the Programs tab. In the E-mail field, select Microsoft Outlook. Click OK.

If you want to send a copy (or copies) of the e-mail to other recipients, also complete the Cc ('Carbon' or 'Courtesy' copy) section.

You may have to configure Outlook 2000's Remote Mail facility before you can send e-mail. See page 185.

You can use Word to write and send e-mail messages (provided you've also installed Outlook).

Pull down the File menu and click New. In the New dialog, activate the General tab. Double-click the E-mail Message icon. Now do the following:

1 Type in the recipient's e-mail address

2 Type in a subject

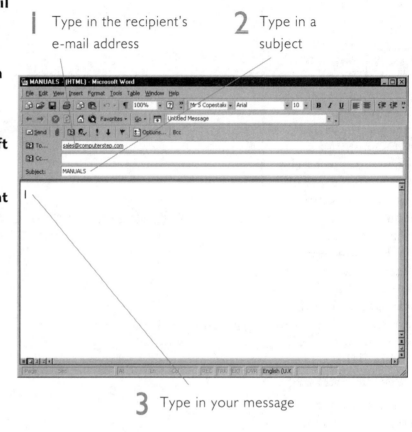

3 Type in your message

4 Click this toolbar button: ⬛ Send

To e-mail a *pre-written* document, click this button:

in the Standard toolbar. Then follow steps 1, 2 and 4 above.

Moving around in documents

To move to the location where you last made an amendment, press Shift+F5. You can do this as many as three times in succession.

When you drag the box on the vertical scroll bar, Word 2000 displays a page indicator (magnified in the illustration) showing which page you're up to. (The page indicator doesn't appear in Web Layout view.)

You can use the following to move through Word 2000 documents:

- keystrokes

- the vertical/horizontal scroll bars

- the Go To section of the Find and Replace dialog

The keystroke route

Word implements the standard Windows direction keys. Use the left, right, up and down cursor keys in the usual way. Additionally, Home, End, Page Up and Page Down work normally.

The scroll bar route

Use your mouse to perform any of the following actions:

Click anywhere here to jump to another location in the document

Click anywhere here to jump to another location in the document

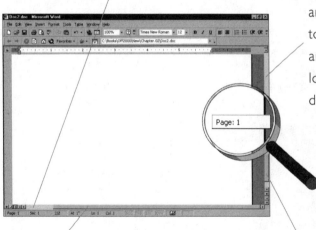

Drag this to the left or right to extend the viewing area

Drag this up or down to move through the active document

The dialog route

You can use the Go To tab in the Find and Replace dialog to move to a variety of document locations. These include:

- pages (probably the most common)

- lines

- pictures

Pull down the Edit menu and click Go To. Now do the following:

You can use a keyboard shortcut to launch the Go To dialog: simply press Ctrl+G.

| Click the location type you want to go to   3 Click here

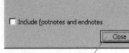

To have Word count the words in the active document, pull down the Tools menu and click Word Count. This is the result:

2 Type in the specific location reference (e.g. a number if you selected 'Page' in step 1)

There are some useful refinements:

- You can enter *relative* movements in step 2. For example, if you want to move seventeen pages back from the present location, type in -17. Or +5 to move five pages forward...

- To move to the next or previous instance of the specified location (i.e. without specifying a reference), omit step 2. In step 3, the dialog is now slightly different; click Next or Previous, as appropriate. Click Close when you've finished.

Click here to close

Views

Word 2000 also provides another view which you'll use frequently: Print Preview.

See pages 96–99 for more information.

Word 2000 lets you examine your work in various ways, according to the approach you need. It calls these 'views'. The principal views are:

Normal

Normal View – the default – is used for basic text editing. In Normal View, text formatting elements are still visible; for instance, coloured, emboldened or italicised text displays faithfully. However, little attempt is made to show document structure or layout (for example, headers/footers, page boundaries and most pictures are invisible). For these reasons, Normal View is quick and easy to use. It's suitable for bulk text entry and editing, but not recommended for use with graphics.

Print Layout

Print Layout view works like Normal view, with one exception: the positioning of items on the page is reproduced accurately. Headers/footers and pictures are visible, and can be edited directly; margins display faithfully.

In Print Layout view, the screen is updated more slowly. Use it when your document is nearing completion.

Web Layout

In Web layout view, Web pages are optimised so that they appear as they will when published to the Web or an Intranet. Effects which are often used on the Web display (e.g. backgrounds and AutoShapes).

The stationery shown in the illustration can be found in the following folder:
Program Files\Common Files\Microsoft Shared\Stationery

(When viewed in Normal or Print Layout views, this file appears blank.)

In Outlook, you can use stationeries to make e-mail more visually attractive (but only if you aren't using Word 2000 as your e-mail editor).

It's a Party and You're Invited

Day:

Time:

Word 2000 displaying one of Outlook's HTML stationeries

When Full Screen view is active, you lose access to toolbars and scroll bars. However, you can still access the menus by using the keyboard (e.g. Alt+F to launch the File menu).

This feature – as part of Office 2000's Install on Demand – may not be installed. If it isn't, Word launches a special message (if the Assistant is on-screen – if not, a standard message appears):

⚠ Microsoft Word

This feature is not currently installed. Would you like to install it now?

Yes   No

Click Yes and follow the on-screen instructions. Then carry out steps 1–3.

Full Screen

Unless you have a particularly large monitor, you'll probably find that there are times when your screen is too cluttered. Full Screen view hides all standard screen components in one operation, thereby making more space available for editing.

Use Full Screen view when you need it, as an adjunct to Normal or Print Layout view.

Summarising documents

In effect, Word provides another way to view a document: you can 'summarise' it. When you summarise a document, Word 2000:

- analyses it and allocates a 'score' to each sentence

- allocates a higher score for sentences which contain repeated words

After this, you specify what percentage of the higher-scoring sentences you want to display.

To summarise the active document, pull down the Tools menu and click AutoSummarize. Word 2000 carries out the initial analysis. When it's completed, do the following:

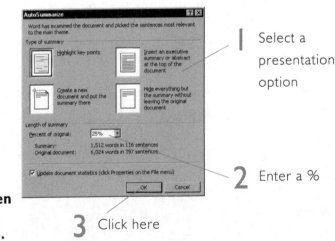

1 Select a presentation option

2 Enter a %

3 Click here

Implementing views

Switching to Normal, Web Layout or Print Layout views

Pull down the View menu and do the following:

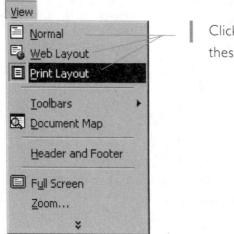

Click one of these

Switching to Full Screen view

Pull down the View menu and do the following:

 To leave Full Screen view, press Esc or do the following in the on-screen toolbar:

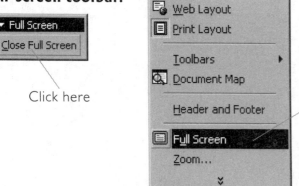

Click here

Click here

Changing zoom levels

The ability to vary the level of magnification for the active document is often useful. Sometimes, it's helpful to 'zoom out' (i.e. decrease the magnification) so that you can take an overview; at other times, you'll need to 'zoom in' (increase the magnification) to work in greater detail. Word 2000 lets you do either of these very easily.

You can do any of the following:

• choose from preset zoom levels (e.g. 100%, 75%)

• specify your own zoom percentage

• choose Many Pages, to view a specific number of pages

Setting the zoom level

The Zoom dialog varies slightly according to which view you're using.

Pull down the View menu and click Zoom. Now carry out steps 1 or 2 (to specify a zoom %) OR 3 & 4 (to specify a group of pages). Finally, in either case, follow step 5.

The Preview section on the right provides an indication of what the selected view level looks like.

Click a preset zoom level

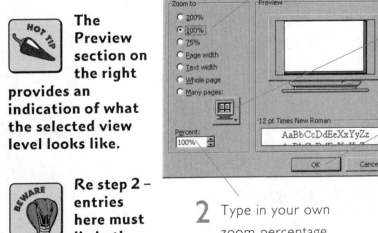

3 Click here

5 Click here

2 Type in your own zoom percentage

Re step 2 – entries here must lie in the range 10%–500%.

4 Click a multiple-page view

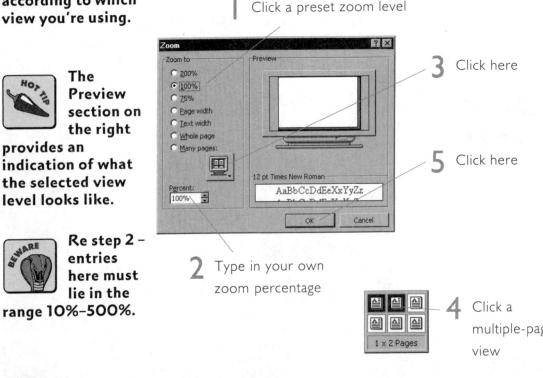

Formatting text – an overview

Word 2000 lets you format text in a variety of ways. Broadly, however, text formatting can be divided into two overall categories:

You can have Word 2000 format the active document automatically.

Pull down the Tools menu and click AutoCorrect. In the AutoCorrect dialog, click the AutoFormat tab. Specify the type(s) of formatting you want applied. Finally, click OK.

Character formatting

Character formatting is concerned with altering the *appearance* of selected text. Examples include:

- changing the font and type size

- colouring text

- changing the font style (bold, italic etc.)

- underlining text

- applying font effects (superscript, subscript, small caps etc.)

Character formatting is a misnomer in one sense: it can also be applied to specific paragraphs of text.

Paragraph formatting

Paragraph formatting has to do with the structuring and layout of paragraphs of text. Examples include:

Whenever you type in Internet paths e.g.: http://www. computerstep.com **(without the break), AutoFormat automatically implements them as hypertext links. This means that clicking an address takes you there (if your Internet link is currently open).**

- specifying paragraph indents

- specifying paragraph alignment (e.g. left or right justification)

- specifying paragraph and line spacing

- imposing borders and/or fills on paragraphs

The term "paragraph formatting" is also something of a misnomer in that some of these – for instance, line-spacing – can also be applied to the whole of the active document rather than selected paragraphs.

Changing the font or type size

Character formatting can be changed in two ways:

- from within the Font dialog

- (to a lesser extent) by using the Formatting toolbar

Word 2000 uses standard Windows procedures for text selection.

Applying a new font/type size – the dialog route

First, select the text whose typeface and/or type size you want to amend. Pull down the Format menu and click Font. Now carry out step 1. Perform step 2 and/or 3. Finally, carry out step 4:

1 Ensure the Font tab is active

Re step 3 – as well as whole point sizes, you can also enter half-point increments. For instance, Word 2000 will accept:
10, 10.5 or 11
but not:
10.7 or 10.85.

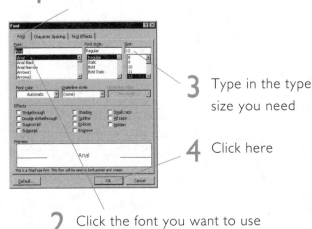

3 Type in the type size you need

4 Click here

2 Click the font you want to use

If the Formatting toolbar isn't currently visible, pull down the View menu and click Toolbars, Formatting.

Applying a new font/type size – the toolbar route

Make sure the Formatting toolbar is visible. Now select the text you want to amend and do the following:

Click here; select the font you want to use in the drop-down list

Type in the type size you need and press Enter

Changing text colour

First, select the text you want to alter. Pull down the Format menu and click Font. Now do the following:

Ensure the Font tab is active

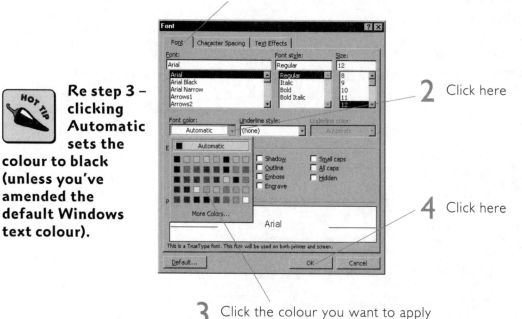

2 Click here

4 Click here

Re step 3 – clicking Automatic sets the colour to black (unless you've amended the default Windows text colour).

3 Click the colour you want to apply

Verifying current text formatting

If you're in any doubt about what character/paragraph formatting attributes are associated with text, press Shift+F1. Now click in the text. This is the result:

Paragraph Formatting
Paragraph Style: Indent: Left 0" Right 0" Centered, Keep with next, Level 1

Direct:

Font Formatting
Paragraph Style: Font: Arial, English (U.K.)
Character Style:
Direct: Font: 15 pt

Verifying text formatting

Press Esc to return to normal text editing.

Changing the font style

Don't confuse font styles with text styles (text styles are groups of formatting commands and are much more diverse – see pages 77–81).

The default font style is Regular. The additional font styles you can use depend on the typeface. For example, 'Times New Roman' has 'Bold', 'Italic' and 'Bold Italic'. 'Arial Rounded MT Bold', on the other hand, merely has 'Bold' and 'Bold Italic'.

You can use the Font dialog or the Formatting toolbar to change font styles.

Amending the font style – the dialog route

First, select the text whose style you want to change. Then pull down the Format menu and click Font. Do the following:

To underline text, click here: select an underlining type in the list.

Ensure the Font tab is active

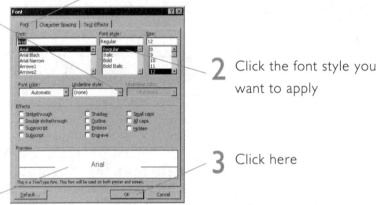

2 Click the font style you want to apply

The Preview section provides an indication of what the amendments you make will look like.

3 Click here

Amending the font style – the toolbar route

First, select the relevant text. Ensure the Formatting toolbar is visible. Then do any of the following:

If the Formatting toolbar isn't visible, pull down the View menu and click Toolbars, Formatting.

Click here to embolden the text

Click here to italicise it

Click here to underline it

Font effects

The following are the principal font effects:

- Strikethrough – e.g. ~~font effect~~

- Superscript – e.g. f$^{\text{ont effect}}$

- Subscript – e.g. f$_{\text{ont effect}}$

- All Caps – e.g. FONT EFFECT

- Small Caps – e.g. FONT EFFECT

In addition, you can mark text as hidden, which means that it doesn't display on screen or print.

Applying font effects

First, select the relevant text. Pull down the Format menu and click Font. Then carry out the following steps:

Ensure the Font tab is active

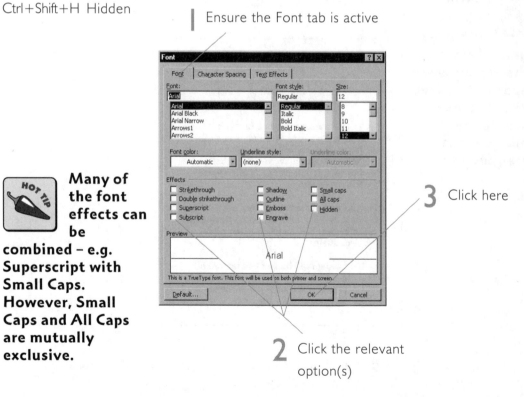

3 Click here

2 Click the relevant option(s)

Indenting paragraphs – an overview

Indents are a crucial component of document layout. For instance, in most document types, indenting the first line of paragraphs (i.e. moving it inwards away from the left page margin) makes the text much more legible.

You can achieve a similar effect by using tabs. However, indents are easier to apply (and amend subsequently).

Other document types – e.g. bibliographies – can use the following:

- negative indents (where the direction of indent is towards and beyond the left margin)

- hanging indents (where the first line is unaltered, while subsequent lines are indented)

- full indents (where the entire paragraph is indented away from the left and/or the right margins)

Don't confuse indents with page margins. Margins are the gap between the edge of the page and the text area; indents define the distance between the margins and text.

Some of the potential indent combinations are shown in the illustration below:

> This paragraph has a full left and right indent. It's best, however, not to overdo the extent of the indent: 0.35 inches is often more than adequate.
>
>   This paragraph has a first-line indent. This type of indent is suitable for most document types. It's best, however, not to overdo the extent of the indent: 0.35 inches is often more than adequate.
>
> This paragraph has a negative left indent. It's best, however, not to overdo the extent of the indent: 0.35 inches is often more than adequate.
>
> This paragraph has a hanging indent. It's best, however, not to overdo the extent of the indent: 0.35 inches is often more than adequate.

left and right indent

first-line indent

negative left indent

hanging indent

Left margin (inserted for illustration purposes)

Right margin (inserted for illustration purposes)

Applying indents to paragraphs

Paragraphs can be indented from within the Paragraph dialog or (to an extent) by using the Formatting toolbar.

Indenting text – the dialog route

First, select the paragraph(s) you want to indent. Pull down the Format menu and click Paragraph. Now follow step 1 below. If you want a left indent, carry out step 2. For a right indent, follow step 3. To achieve a first-line or hanging indent, follow steps 4 and 5. Finally, irrespective of the indent type, carry out step 6.

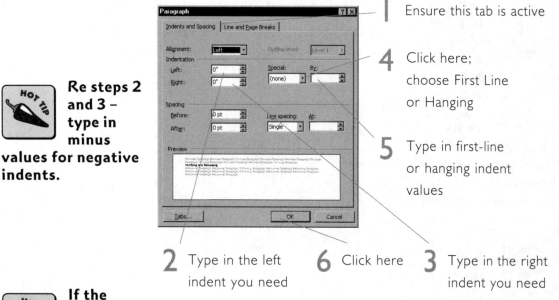

1 Ensure this tab is active

4 Click here; choose First Line or Hanging

5 Type in first-line or hanging indent values

Re steps 2 and 3 – type in minus values for negative indents.

2 Type in the left indent you need

6 Click here

3 Type in the right indent you need

If the Formatting toolbar isn't visible, pull down the View menu and click Toolbars, Formatting.

Indenting text – the toolbar route

First, select the relevant paragraph(s). Ensure the Formatting toolbar is visible. Then click one of these:

Indents the paragraph(s) to the next tab stop

Indents the paragraph(s) to the previous tab stop

Aligning paragraphs

You can adjust alignment from within the Paragraph dialog, or by the use of the Formatting toolbar.

Word 2000 supports the following types of alignment:

Left alignment
Text is flush with the left page margin.

Right alignment
Text is flush with the right page margin.

Justification
Text is flush with the left *and* right page margins.

Centred
Text is placed evenly between the left/right page margins.

Aligning text – the dialog route
First, select the paragraph(s) you want to align. Pull down the Format menu and click Paragraph. Now:

Re the HOT TIP below – if you've used the Right Align or Justify buttons before, Word 2000 may have promoted them to the main body of the Formatting toolbar.

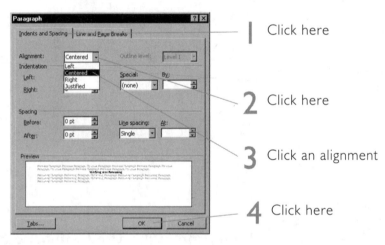

1 Click here

2 Click here

3 Click an alignment

4 Click here

To right-align or justify the selected text, click » on the right of the toolbar. In the flyout, click one of these:

Right align

Justify

Aligning text – the toolbar route
Select the relevant paragraph(s). Then click one of these:

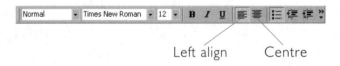

Left align   Centre

Specifying paragraph spacing

As a general rule, set low paragraph spacing settings: a little goes a long way.

Word 2000 lets you customise the vertical space before and/or after specific text paragraphs. This is a useful device for increasing text legibility.

By default, Word defines paragraph spacing – like type sizes – in point sizes. However, if you want you can enter measurements in different units. To do this, apply any of the following suffixes to values you enter:

- in – for inches (e.g. '2 in')
- cm – for centimetres (e.g. '5 cm')
- pi – for picas (e.g. '14 pi')
- px – for pixels (e.g. '50 px' – about ½ inch)

The following definitions should be useful:

- Picas are an alternative measure in typography: one pica is almost equivalent to one-sixth inch. Picas are often used to define line length

- Pixels (a contraction of 'picture elements') are the smallest components of the picture on a computer monitor

Applying paragraph spacing

First, select the paragraph you want to indent. Pull down the Format menu and click Paragraph. Now carry out the steps below:

Ensure the Indents and Spacing tab is active

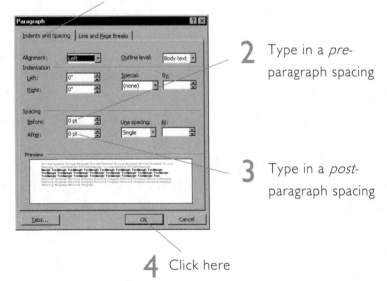

2 Type in a *pre*-paragraph spacing

3 Type in a *post*-paragraph spacing

4 Click here

Line spacing – an overview

Line spacing is also known as leading (pronounced 'ledding').

It's often necessary to amend line spacing. This is the vertical distance between individual lines of text, or more accurately between the baseline (the imaginary line on which text appears to sit) of one line and the baseline of the previous.

Word 2000 lets you apply a variety of line spacing settings:

Single

Word 2000 separates each line of type by an amount which is slightly more than the type size. For example, if the text is in 12 points, the gap between lines is just over 12 points. Newspapers, particularly, use single line spacing.

This is Word 2000's default.

1.5 Lines

150% of single line spacing.

Double

200% of single line spacing. Manuscripts of all descriptions are nearly always prepared with double line spacing.

At Least

Sets the minimum line height at the value you specify; Word 2000 can adjust the line spacing to fit the constituent character sizes.

Exactly

Sets the value you specify as an unvarying line height: Word 2000 cannot adjust it.

Multiple

Sets line height as a multiple of single-spaced text. For example, specifying '3.5' here initiates a line height of 3.5 lines.

Adjusting line spacing

First, select the relevant paragraph(s). Then move the mouse pointer over them and right-click. Do the following:

If you've just created a new document, you can set the line spacing *before* you begin to enter text. With the insertion point at the start of the document, follow the procedures outlined here.

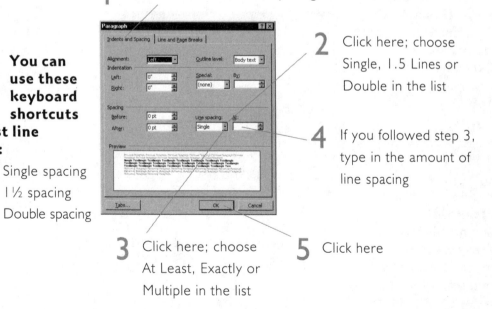

Click here

Now perform step 1 below. If you want to apply a preset spacing, follow step 2. To implement your own spacing, carry out steps 3 and 4 instead. Finally, follow step 5:

1 Ensure the Indents and Spacing tab is active

2 Click here; choose Single, 1.5 Lines or Double in the list

4 If you followed step 3, type in the amount of line spacing

You can use these keyboard shortcuts to adjust line spacing:

Ctrl+1   Single spacing
Ctrl+5   1½ spacing
Ctrl+2   Double spacing

3 Click here; choose At Least, Exactly or Multiple in the list

5 Click here

Paragraph borders

By default, Word 2000 does not border paragraph text. However, you can apply a wide selection of borders if you want. You can specify:

You can also border selected text *within* a paragraph. However, the Borders tab is then slightly different (e.g. you can't deselect the border for specific sides).

- the type and thickness of the border
- how many sides the border should have
- the border colour
- whether the text is shadowed or in 3-D
- the distance of the border from the text

Applying a border

First, select the paragraph(s) you want to border. Then pull down the Format menu and click Borders and Shading. Carry out step 1 below. Now carry out steps 2–5, as appropriate. Finally, perform step 6:

To set the distance from the border to the enclosed text, click Options. Insert the relevant distances and click OK. Then follow step 6.

Use step 5 to deselect the top, bottom, left or right paragraph borders. If you want to deselect more than one, repeat step 5 as often as necessary.

1 Ensure the Borders tab is active

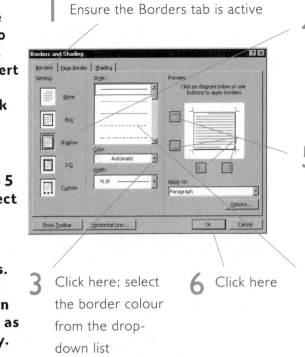

4 Click a border option to border all four sides of the text

5 Optional – click one or more sides (see the DON'T FORGET tip)

3 Click here; select the border colour from the drop-down list

6 Click here

2 Click a line type

Paragraph fills

By default, Word 2000 does not apply a fill to text paragraphs. However, you can do the following if you want:

- specify a percentage fill e.g. 20% (light grey) or 85% (very dark grey)

- apply a simple pattern, if required

- specify a background fill colour

- specify a pattern colour

Applying a fill

First, select the paragraph(s) you want to fill. Then pull down the Format menu and click Borders and Shading. Now carry out step 1 below. Follow steps 2, 3 or 4 as appropriate. Finally, carry out step 5:

Ensure the Shading tab is active

4 Click a background fill colour

Re steps 3 and 4 – you can achieve unique blends by applying different pattern and background colours.

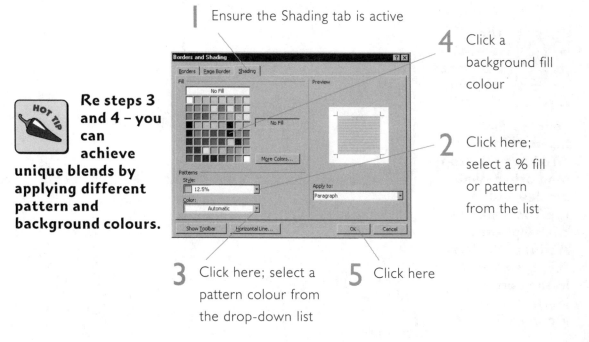

2 Click here; select a % fill or pattern from the list

3 Click here; select a pattern colour from the drop-down list

5 Click here

Working with tabs

Tabs are a means of indenting the first line of text paragraphs (you can also use indents for this purpose – see pages 58–59).

When you press the Tab key while the text-insertion point is at the start of a paragraph, the text in the first line jumps to the next tab stop – see the illustration below:

Never use the Space Bar to indent paragraphs: spaces vary in size according to the typeface and type size applying to specific paragraphs, and therefore give uneven results.

The first tab stop

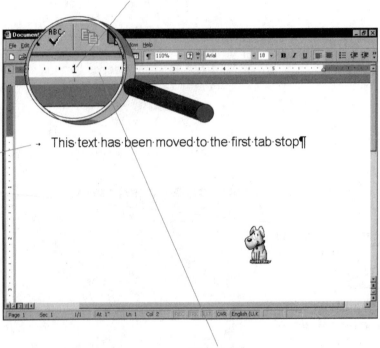

This text has been moved to the first tab stop¶

The Ruler

The symbol on the left of the text:

➡

denotes the inserted tab.

To have tab stops (and other symbols) display, pull down the Tools menu and click Options. Activate the View tab, then select All in the Formatting marks section. Finally, click OK.

Inserting tabs is a useful way to increase the legibility of your text. By default, Word 2000 inserts tab stops automatically every half an inch. If you want, you can enter new or revised tab stop positions individually and with great precision.

Setting tab stops

First, select the paragraph(s) in which you need to set tab stops. Pull down the Format menu and click Tabs. Now carry out step 1 below. If you want to implement a new default tab stop position, follow step 2. If, on the other hand, you need to set up individual tab stops, carry out steps 3 AND 4 as often as necessary. Finally, in either case, follow step 5 to confirm your changes.

When you've performed steps 3 & 4, the individual tab stop position appears here:

2 Type in the new tab stop default (e.g. 0.35")

4 Click here

5 Click here

To display or hide the Ruler (see page 66), pull down the View menu and click Ruler.

3 Type in a single tab stop position

| Click here to remove all existing tab stop positions

Tabs

Tab stop position: 0.35" 0.35"

Default tab stops:

Alignment: Left, Center, Right, Decimal, Bar

Leader: 1 None, 2 ......, 3 ------, 4 ___

Tab stops to be cleared:

Set   Clear   Clear All

OK   Cancel

Searching for text

Word 2000 lets you search for specific text within the active document. Even better, however, you can also search for character or paragraph formatting, either separately from the text search or at the same time.

For example, you can if you want have Word locate all instances of the word 'information'. Or you could have it find all italicised words, whatever they are. Similarly, you could have it flag all instances of '*information*'.

You can also:

- limit the search to words which match the case of the text you specify (e.g. if you search for 'Man', Word will not flag 'man' or 'MAN')

- limit the search to whole words (e.g. if you search for 'nation', Word will not flag 'international')

- have Word search for word forms (e.g. if you look for 'began', Word will also stop at 'begin', 'begun' and 'beginning')

- have Word search for homophones (e.g. if you look for 'there', Word will flag 'their')

Follow step 2 to locate specific formatting. In the extended dialog which launches, click Format. Word 2000 launches a menu; click the relevant entry. Then complete the dialog which appears in the normal way. Finally, follow step 3 to begin the search.

Initiating a text search

Pull down the Edit menu and click Find. Now do the following:

| Type in the text you want to find

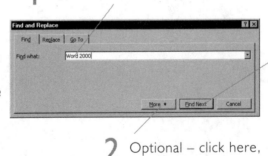

3 Click here to start the search

2 Optional – click here, then see the tip

Replacing text

Word 2000 replaces some words/phrases automatically as you type (e.g. 'accross' becomes 'across'). This is called AutoCorrect, and works with multiple languages (if you've set up Office to work with them – see pages 32–33).

To add your own substitutions, pull down the Tools menu and click AutoCorrect. In the Replace field, insert the *incorrect* word; in the With field, type in the *correct* version. Click OK.

When you follow step 3, Word launches a menu; click the relevant entry. Then complete the dialog which appears in the normal way. Finally, carry out step 5 OR 6, as appropriate.

When you've located text and/or formatting, you can have Word 2000 replace it automatically with the text and/or formatting of your choice.

You can customise find-and-replace operations with the same parameters as a simple Find operation. For example, you can have Word find every occurrence of 'information' and replace it with '*information*', or even '*data*'...

Initiating a find-and-replace operation

First pull down the Edit menu and click Replace. In the Find and Replace dialog, click More. Now follow steps 1 and 2 below. Carry out steps 3 and/or 4, as appropriate. Finally, follow either step 5 OR 6:

1 Type in the text you want to find

2 Type in the replacement text

5 Click here to replace the first instance of the specified text

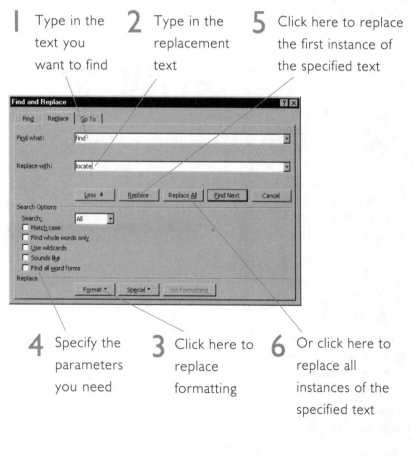

4 Specify the parameters you need

3 Click here to replace formatting

6 Or click here to replace all instances of the specified text

Working with headers

You can have Word 2000 print text at the top of each page within a document; this area is called the 'header'. In the same way, you can have text printed at the base of each page (the 'footer'). Headers and footers are printed within the top and bottom page margins, respectively.

To edit an existing header, simply follow the procedures outlined on the right; in step 1, amend the current header text as necessary.

When you create a header, Word automatically switches the active document to Print Layout view and displays the Header and Footer toolbar.

Inserting a header

Move to the start of your document. Pull down the View menu and click Header and Footer. Do any of the following:

Header text can be formatted in the normal way. For instance, you can apply a new font and/or type size...

1 Type in the Header text

4 Click here to return to normal document editing

You can have Word 2000 insert a special code which automatically inserts the page number in the header – see step 2.

2 Click here to insert a page number code

3 Optional – click here to move to the header on the next page

Working with footers

To edit an existing footer, simply follow the procedures outlined on the right; in step 1, amend the current footer text as necessary.

When you create a footer, Word 2000 automatically switches the active document to Print Layout view and displays the Header and Footer toolbar.

Inserting a footer

Move to the start of your document. Pull down the View menu and click Header and Footer. Word launches the Header and Footer toolbar over the footer area. To create a footer, do the following:

Click here

Footer text can be formatted in the normal way. For instance, you can apply a new font and/or type size...

Word 2000 moves to the footer area. Do any of the following:

2 Click here to insert a page number code

3 Optional – click here to move to the footer on the next page

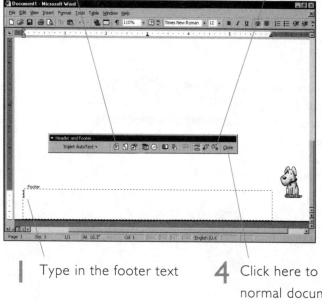

You can have Word insert a special code which automatically inserts the page number in the footer – see step 2.

| Type in the footer text

4 Click here to return to normal document editing

Inserting bookmarks

In computer terms, a bookmark is a marker inserted to enable you to find a given location in a document easily and quickly.

Creating a bookmark

Place the insertion point where you want the bookmark inserted. Pull down the Insert menu and click Bookmark. Now do the following:

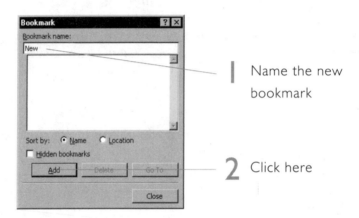

I Name the new bookmark

2 Click here

Jumping to a bookmark

Pull down the Insert menu and click Bookmark. Now do the following:

To delete a bookmark, carry out step 1 on the immediate right. Click this button:

Delete

then follow step 3.

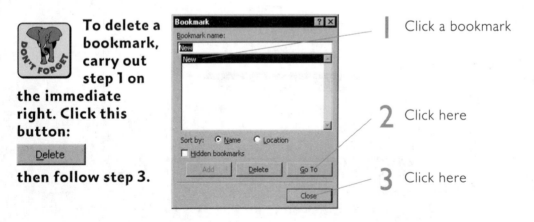

I Click a bookmark

2 Click here

3 Click here

Inserting hyperlinks

You can insert hyperlinks into Word documents. Hyperlinks are text or graphics linked to:

To amend a bookmark hyperlink, place the insertion point within it (for text hyperlinks) or select the picture (for picture hyperlinks). Follow steps 1–2. In step 3, make the necessary changes. Finally, carry out step 4.

- another location (e.g. a pre-inserted bookmark) in the same document, or;

- a document on the World Wide Web or an Intranet

Creating a hyperlink to a bookmark

Select the text or graphic you want to be the source of the link. Pull down the Insert menu and do the following:

Click here

To delete a bookmark hyperlink, place the insertion point within it (for text hyperlinks) or select the picture (for picture hyperlinks). Follow steps 1–2. Now click this button:

Remove Link

2 Click here

3 Select a bookmark or document location

4 Click here

Creating a hyperlink to a Web or Intranet HTML file

Select the text or graphic you want to be the source of the link. Pull down the Insert menu and do the following:

To amend a document hyperlink, place the insertion point within it (for text hyperlinks) or select the picture (for picture hyperlinks). Follow steps 1–2. In step 3, make the necessary changes. Finally, carry out step 4.

Click here

To delete a document hyperlink, place the insertion point within it (for text hyperlinks) or select the picture (for picture hyperlinks). Follow steps 1–2. Now click this button:

Remove Link

2 Click here

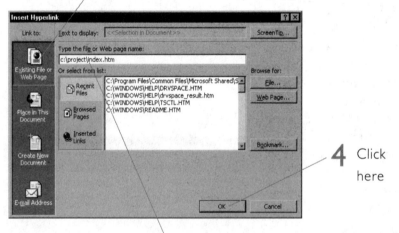

4 Click here

3 Type in a document address

Activating hyperlinks

To jump to one of the following:

- a bookmark (see page 72)

- a linked World Wide Web or Intranet document

do the following:

> Here, a hyperlink to Computer Step's Web site (http://www.computerstep.com) is being activated – notice that the mouse pointer changes to a hand

To activate a hyperlink to a World Wide Web document, first ensure your Internet connection is live.

Note that inserted text hyperlinks are:

- underlined
- coloured blue

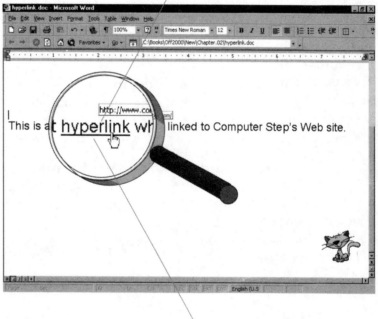

Click any hyperlink

When you activate a hyperlink to a Web or Intranet document, Word 2000 opens a read-only version of it.

Undo and redo

Word lets you reverse – 'undo' – just about any editing operation. If, subsequently, you decide that you do want to proceed with an operation that you've reversed, you can 'redo' it.

You can even undo or redo a series of operations in one go.

You can undo and redo actions in the following ways (in descending order of complexity):

- via the keyboard

- from within the Edit menu

- from within the Standard toolbar

Using the keyboard

Simply press Ctrl+Z to undo an action, or Ctrl+Y to reinstate it.

Using the Edit menu

Pull down the Edit menu and click Undo... or Redo... as appropriate (the ellipses denote the precise nature of the action to be reversed or reinstated).

Using the Standard toolbar

Carry out the following action to undo an action (see the DON'T FORGET tip for how to reinstate it):

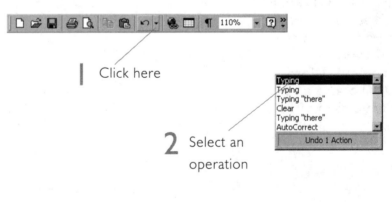

Click here

2 Select an operation

Text styles – an overview

The basic template also has a number of Internet-related **styles e.g.:**

- HTML Address
- HTML Keyboard
- HTML Sample

These styles use Times New Roman **or** Courier **as their base typefaces, and are particularly suitable for use in Web documents.**

You can easily create (and apply) your own styles – see pages 79–80.

There are also more specialised styles in NORMAL.DOT. **These relate to:**

- generic, bulleted and numbered lists
- titles and subtitles
- page numbers
- hyperlinks which have been clicked (activated)

Styles are named collections of associated formatting commands.

The advantage of using styles is that you can apply more than one formatting enhancement to selected text in one go. Once a style is in place, you can change one or more elements of it and have Word 2000 apply the amendments automatically throughout the whole of the active document.

Generally, new documents you create in Word 2000 are based on the NORMAL.DOT template and have a variety of pre-defined styles. Some of the main ones include:

Body Text	used for specialised body text
Body Text 2	used for specialised body text
Body Text 3	used for specialised body text
Normal	used for standard body text
Default Paragraph Font	used for paragraph text
Heading 1	used for headings
Heading 2	used for headings
Heading 3	used for headings
Heading 4	used for headings
Heading 5	used for headings
Heading 6	used for headings
Heading 7	used for headings
Heading 8	used for headings
Heading 9	used for headings
Hyperlink	used to denote inactive hyperlinks

Finding out which text style is in force

If you're in any doubt about which style is associated with text, you can arrange to view style names in a special pane to the left of text.

You can only view the Style pane in Normal view.

Pull down the Tools menu and click Options. Do the following:

Activate this tab

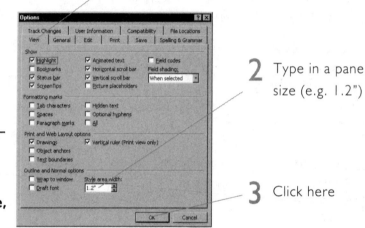

2 Type in a pane size (e.g. 1.2")

Re step 2 – if you no longer wish to view the Style Pane, reset the pane size to 0".

3 Click here

To view the Style pane, pull down the View menu and click Normal:

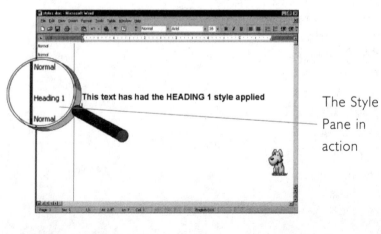

This text has had the HEADING 1 style applied

The Style Pane in action

Creating a text style

The easiest way to create a style is to:

A.   apply the appropriate formatting enhancements to specific text and then select it

B.   tell Word to save this formatting as a style

First, carry out A. above. Then pull down the Format menu and click Style. Now do the following:

Here, Word previews the effect of applying a style:

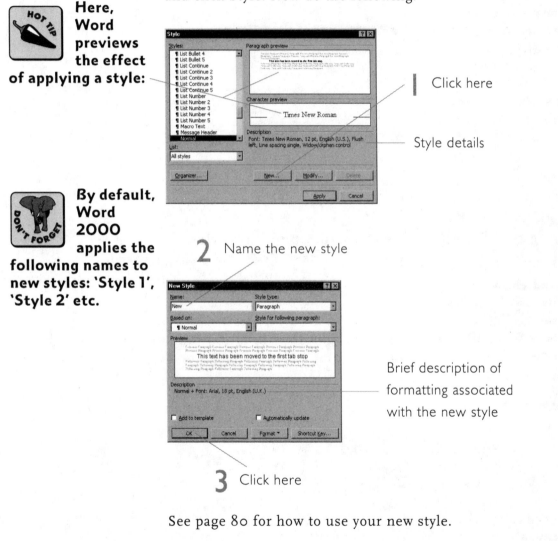

Click here

Style details

By default, Word 2000 applies the following names to new styles: 'Style 1', 'Style 2' etc.

2 Name the new style

Brief description of formatting associated with the new style

3 Click here

See page 80 for how to use your new style.

Applying a text style

You can delete user-created styles, if necessary. Follow step 1. Click the Delete button. In the message which launches, click Yes. Finally, click the Close button.

(When you delete a style, any text associated with it automatically has the Normal style applied to it.)

Word 2000 makes applying styles easy.

First, select the text you want to apply the style to. Or, if you only want to apply it to a single paragraph, place the insertion point inside it. Pull down the Format menu and click Style. Now do the following:

Click a style

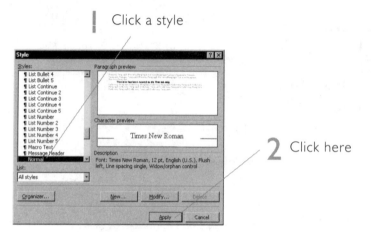

2 Click here

Re the shortcut – if you haven't used the Style button recently, it may be in the toolbar flyout. If so, click

to access it.

Shortcut for applying styles

Word 2000 makes it even easier to apply styles if you currently have the Formatting toolbar on-screen. (If you haven't, pull down the View menu and click Toolbars, Formatting.)

Select the text you want to apply the style to. Refer to the Formatting toolbar then do the following:

Click here in the Style button

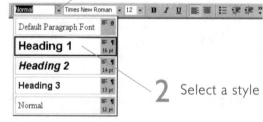

2 Select a style

Re step 2 – entries in the Style drop-down list display with accurate formatting.

Amending a text style

Re step 1 – if you haven't used the Style button recently, it may be in the toolbar flyout. If so, click

≫ ▼

to access it.

The easiest way to modify an existing style is to:

A. apply the appropriate formatting enhancements to specific text and then select it

B. use the Formatting toolbar to tell Word 2000 to assign the selected formatting to the associated style

First, carry out A. above. Refer to the Formatting toolbar then do the following:

You can have Word 2000 update a style automatically whenever you amend the formatting of text to which it has been applied.

Pull down the Format menu and click Styles. In the Styles field, select a style. Click this button:

1 Click here in the Style button

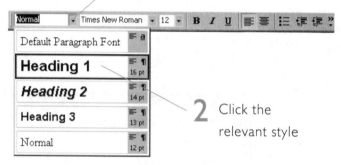

2 Click the relevant style

Word 2000 launches a special message. Do the following:

3 Make sure this is selected

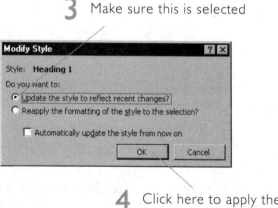

In the Modify Style dialog, ensure Automatically Update is selected. Click OK. Back in the Style dialog, click Apply or Close, as appropriate.

4 Click here to apply the specified amendments to the style

Spell- and grammar-checking

By default, Word 2000 checks spelling and grammar simultaneously.

Word 2000 lets you check text in two ways:

- on-the-fly, as you type in text

- separately, after the text has been entered

Checking text on-the-fly

This is the default. When automatic checking is in force, Word 2000 flags words it doesn't agree with, using a red underline (in the case of misspellings) and a green line (for grammatical errors). If the word or phrase is wrong, right-click in it. Then carry out steps 1, 2 or 3:

Re step 2 – if Word has flagged a spelling error, you have an extra option. Click Add if:

1. the flagged word is correct, and

2. you want Word to remember it in future spell-checks (by adding it to your User dictionary)

1 Word often provides a list of alternatives. If one is correct, click it; the flagged word is replaced with the correct version

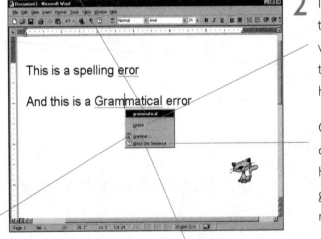

2 If you want the flagged word/phrase to stand, click here

Optional – click here for help with grammatical rules

Here, we're correcting a grammatical error. If a spelling error has been flagged, this section of the menu shows:

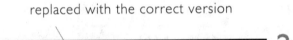

3 If the flagged word is wrong but can't be corrected now, click here and complete the resulting dialog (see over)

Disabling on-the-fly checking

Pull down the Tools menu and click Options. Activate the Spelling and Grammar tab, then deselect Check spelling as you type and/or Check grammar as you type. Click OK.

Word makes use of two separate dictionaries. One – CUSTOM.DIC – is yours. When you click the Add button (see the tip below), the flagged word is stored in CUSTOM.DIC and recognised in future checking sessions.

If you're correcting a spelling error, you have two further options:

- Click Add to have the flagged word stored in CUSTOM.DIC (see above), or;

- Click Change All to have Word substitute its suggestion for *all* future instances of the flagged word

Word's Office Assistant explains basic grammatical points here.

Checking text separately

To check all the text within the active document in one go, pull down the Tools menu and click Spelling and Grammar. Word 2000 starts spell- and grammar-checking the document from the beginning. When it encounters a word or phrase it doesn't recognise, Word flags it and produces a special dialog (see below). Usually, it provides alternative suggestions; if one of these is correct, you can opt to have it replace the flagged word. You can do this singly (i.e. just this instance is replaced) or globally (where all future instances – within the current checking session – are replaced).

Alternatively, you can have Word ignore *this* instance of the flagged word, ignore *all* future instances of the word or add the word to CUSTOM.DIC (see the tips). After this, Word resumes checking.

Carry out step 1 below, then follow step 2. Alternatively, carry out step 3 or 4.

1 If one of the suggestions here is correct, click it, then follow step 2

3 Click here to ignore just this instance

4 Click here to ignore all future instances

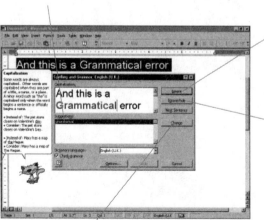

2 Click here to replace this instance

Searching for synonyms

Word 2000 lets you search for synonyms while you're editing the active document. You do this by calling up Word's resident Thesaurus. The Thesaurus categorises words into meanings; each meaning is allocated various synonyms from which you can choose.

 Word 2000's Thesaurus may not be installed (Install on Demand in action).
If it isn't, follow the on-screen instructions after clicking Language, Thesaurus in the Tools menu.

As a bonus, the Thesaurus also supplies antonyms. For example, if you look up 'good' in the Thesaurus (as below), Word lists 'poor' as an antonym.

Using the thesaurus

First, select the word for which you require a synonym or antonym (or simply position the insertion point within it). Pull down the Tools menu and click Language, Thesaurus. Now do the following:

The selected word appears here

 If you've set up Office 2000 to work with specific additional languages (see pages 32–33), Word automatically:

- detects the language being used, and:
- applies the correct proofing tools (spell- and grammar-check, AutoCorrect etc.)

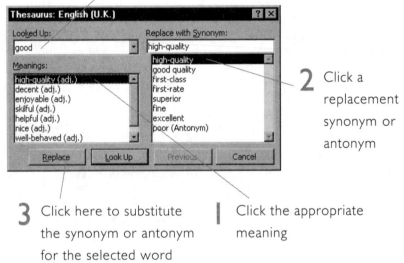

2 Click a replacement synonym or antonym

3 Click here to substitute the synonym or antonym for the selected word

I Click the appropriate meaning

Working with pictures

You can have Word 2000 insert pictures automatically, by using its AutoCorrect feature.

To set up a picture as an AutoCorrect entry, select it. Pull down the Tools menu and click AutoCorrect. In the Replace field, insert the word/phrase you want the picture to replace. Select Formatted text. Click Add, followed by OK.

To insert a picture stored as an AutoCorrect entry, do the following:

1. type in the verbal trigger you set in the HOT TIP above

2. press Space (or any other punctuation). Alternatively, press Enter or Return

Word 2000 lets you add colour and greyscale pictures to the active document. Pictures – also called graphics – include:

- drawings produced in other programs

- clip art

- scanned photographs

Pictures are stored in various third-party formats. These formats are organised into two basic types:

Bitmap images

Bitmaps consist of pixels (dots) arranged in such a way that they form a graphic image. Because of the very nature of bitmaps, the question of 'resolution' – the sharpness of an image expressed in dpi (dots per inch) – is very important. Bitmaps look best if they're displayed at their correct resolution. Word 2000 can manipulate a wide variety of third-party bitmap graphics formats. These include: PCX, TIF, TGA and GIF.

Vector images

You can also insert vector graphics files into Word 2000 documents. Vector images consist of and are defined by algebraic equations. They're less complex than bitmaps and contain less detail. Vector files can also include bitmap information.

Irrespective of the format type, Word 2000 can incorporate pictures with the help of special 'filters'. These are special mini-programs whose job it is to translate third-party formats into a form which Word can use.

Brief notes on picture formats

Graphics formats Word 2000 will accept include the following (the column on the left shows the relevant file suffix):

CGM   Computer Graphics Metafile. A vector format frequently used in the past, especially as a medium for clip-art transmission. Less often used nowadays.

EPS   Encapsulated PostScript. Perhaps the most widely used PostScript format. PostScript combines vector *and* bitmap data very successfully. Incorporates a low-resolution bitmap 'header' for preview purposes.

Two further much-used formats are:

- Windows Bitmap. A popular bitmap format. File suffix: BMP
- Windows Metafile. A frequently used vector format. Used for information exchange between just about all Windows programs. File suffix: WMF

GIF   Graphics Interchange Format. Developed for the on-line transmission of graphics data over the Internet. Just about any Windows program – and a lot more besides – will read GIF. Disadvantage: it can't handle more than 256 colours. Compression is supported.

PCD   (Kodak) PhotoCD. Used primarily to store photographs on CD.

PCX   An old stand-by. Originated with PC Paintbrush, a paint program. Used for years to transfer graphics data between Windows applications.

TGA   Targa. A high-end format, and also a bridge with so-called low-end computers (e.g. Amiga and Atari). Often used in PC and Mac paint and ray-tracing programs because of its high-resolution colour fidelity.

TIFF   Tagged Image File Format. Suffix: TIF. If anything, even more widely used than PCX, across a whole range of platforms and applications.

Inserting pictures

You can use Click and Type to insert pictures in blank page areas.

All clips have associated keywords. You can use these to locate clips.
Click in this field in the Gallery:

Type one or more words...

Now type in one or more keywords. Finally, press Enter – any relevant clips display.

Re step 2 – the Clip Gallery organises clips under overall categories.

To see more Gallery clips, click this:

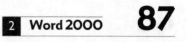

Keep Looking

You can insert pictures in two ways:

- with the Office Clip Gallery

- using a separate dialog

Inserting pictures via the Clip Gallery

First, position the insertion point at the location within the active document where you want to insert the picture. Pull down the Insert menu and click Picture, Clip Art. Do the following:

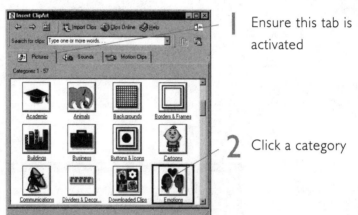

1 Ensure this tab is activated

2 Click a category

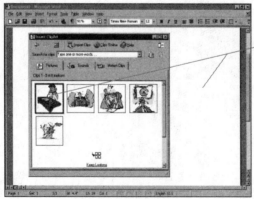

3 Drag a clip into your document

4 Release the mouse button – Word 2000 inserts the picture

You can use Click and Type to insert pictures in blank page areas – see pages 44–45.

Inserting pictures – the dialog route

First, position the insertion point at the location within the active document where you want to insert the picture. Pull down the Insert menu and do the following:

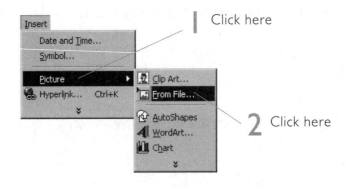

1 Click here

2 Click here

4 Click here. In the drop-down list, click the drive/folder that hosts the picture

Word 2000 provides a preview of what the picture will look like when it's been imported. (See the Preview box on the right of the dialog.)

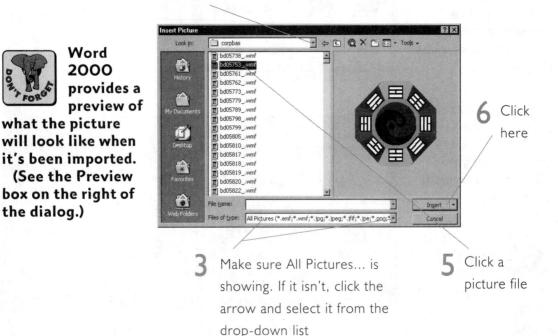

6 Click here

3 Make sure All Pictures... is showing. If it isn't, click the arrow and select it from the drop-down list

5 Click a picture file

Editing pictures

Once you've inserted pictures into a Word 2000 document, you can amend them in a variety of ways. For instance, you can:

- rescale them

- apply a border

- crop them

- move them

To carry out any of these operations, you have to select the relevant picture first. To do this, simply position the mouse pointer over the image and left-click once. Word surrounds the image with eight handles. These are positioned at the four corners, and midway on each side. The illustration below demonstrates these:

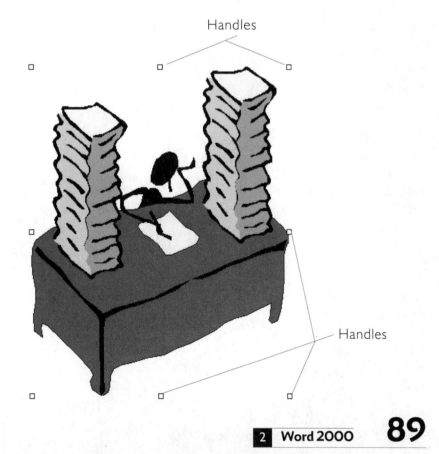

Handles

Handles

Rescaling pictures

To move a picture on the page, select it. Then move the mouse pointer over the picture. Click and hold down the left mouse button; drag the image to a new location. Release the mouse button to confirm the move.

There are two ways in which you can rescale pictures:

- proportionally, where the height/width ratio remains constant

- disproportionately, where the height/width ratio is disrupted (this is sometimes called 'warping' or 'skewing')

To rescale a picture, first select it. Then move the mouse pointer over:

- one of the corner handles, if you want to rescale the image proportionately,

or

- one of the handles in the middle of the sides, if you want to warp it

In either eventuality, the mouse pointer changes to a double-headed arrow. Click and hold down the left mouse button. Drag outwards to increase the image size or inwards to decrease it. Release the mouse button to confirm the change.

To control how text aligns around a picture, select it. Pull down the Format menu and click Picture. In the Format Picture dialog, activate the Layout tab. Now select a text wrap option e.g.:

Here, the image has been skewed to the right

where text aligns around the top and bottom of the image, but not the sides. Finally, click OK.

Bordering pictures

By default, Word 2000 does not apply a border to inserted pictures. However, you can apply a wide selection of borders if you want. You can specify:

- the style and/or thickness of the border

- the border colour

- whether the border is dashed

Applying a border

First, select the picture you want to border. Then pull down the Format menu and click Borders and Shading. Now carry out step 1 below. Perform 2–5, as appropriate. Finally, carry out step 6:

To specify a border width, do the following just before you carry out step 6:

Click here in the Width field; in the list, select a width

Use step 5 to deselect the top, bottom, left or right picture borders. (If you want to deselect more than one, repeat step 5 as often as necessary.)

Ensure the Borders tab is active

4 Click a border option to border all four sides of the image

5 Optional – click one or more sides (see the DON'T FORGET tip)

3 Click here; select the border colour from the drop-down list

6 Click here

2 Click a line type

Cropping pictures

Cropping is the process of trimming the edges off a picture, either to make it fit within a smaller space or to remove parts that are unwanted.

Cropping a picture

First, select the picture you want to crop. Then refer to the Picture toolbar. (If it isn't visible, pull down the View menu and click Toolbars, Picture.) Do the following:

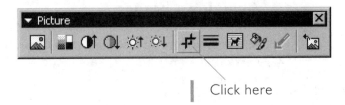

Click here

Now select the picture you want to crop. Move the mouse pointer over one of the available eight handles. Hold down the left mouse button and drag the handle inwards. Release the button to confirm the cropping operation.

When you've carried out step 1, the pointer becomes:

    The Crop pointer

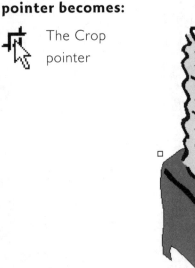

Here, the image has been cropped using the centre-right handle

Page setup – an overview

You can control page layout to a great extent in Word 2000. You can specify:

- the top, bottom, left and/or right page margins

- the distance between the top page edge and the top edge of the header

- the distance between the bottom page edge and bottom edge of the footer

The illustration below shows these page components:

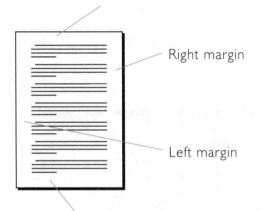

Top margin (including header)

Right margin

Left margin

Bottom margin
(including footer)

You can also specify:

- the page size (irrespective of margins and headers/footers)

- the page orientation ('landscape' or 'portrait')

If none of the supplied page sizes is suitable, you can even customise your own.

Specifying margins

Margin settings are the framework on which indents and tabs are based.

All documents have margins, because printing on the whole of a sheet is both unsightly and – in the case of many printers, since the mechanism has to grip the page – impossible. Documents need a certain amount of 'white space' (the unprinted portion of the page) to balance the areas which contain text and graphics. Without this, they can't be visually effective. As a result, it's important to set margins correctly.

Customising margins

First, position the insertion point at the location within the active document from which you want the new margin(s) to apply. Alternatively, select the relevant portion of your document. Then pull down the File menu and click Page Setup. Now carry out step 1 below. Then follow steps 2–5, as appropriate. Finally, carry out step 6.

| Ensure the Margins tab is active

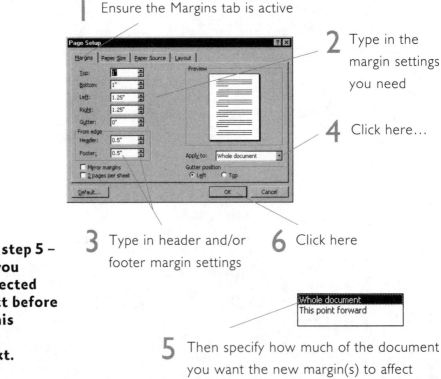

2 Type in the margin settings you need

4 Click here...

3 Type in header and/or footer margin settings

6 Click here

Re step 5 – if you selected text before launching this dialog, click Selected Text.

5 Then specify how much of the document you want the new margin(s) to affect

Specifying the page size

Word 2000 comes with some 17 preset page sizes – for instance, A4, A5 and Letter. These are suitable for most purposes. However, you can also set up your own page definition if you need to.

Whatever the page size, you can have both portrait and landscape pages in the same document.

There are two aspects to every page size: a vertical measurement, and a horizontal measurement. These can be varied according to orientation. There are two possible orientations:

Portrait   Landscape

Re step 2 – to create your own page size, click Custom size. Then type in the desired measurements in the Width and Height fields. Finally, carry out step 4.

Setting the page size

First, position the insertion point at the location within the active document from which you want the new page size to apply. Then pull down the File menu and click Page Setup. Now do the following:

1 Ensure the Paper Size tab is active

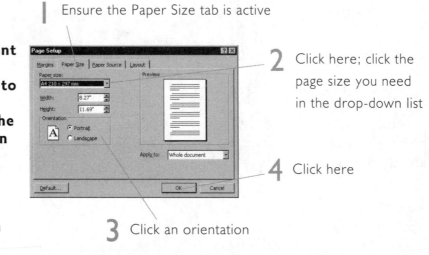

2 Click here; click the page size you need in the drop-down list

4 Click here

If you don't want your changes to affect the entire document, click the 'Apply to:' field. In the list, select a more appropriate option (e.g. This point forward). Finally, perform step 4.

3 Click an orientation

Using Print Preview

You can edit text directly from within Print Preview.

With the magnifying cursor displaying, zoom in on the text you want to edit (see page 97 for how to do this). Click this button in the Print Preview toolbar:

The cursor becomes:

Now click in the text and make the necessary changes.

To leave Print Preview mode, simply press Esc.

Word 2000 provides a special view mode called Print Preview. This displays the active document exactly as it will look when printed. Use Print Preview as a final check just before you print your document.

You can customise the way Print Preview displays your document in various ways. For example, you can:

• zoom in or out on the active page

• specify how many pages display

• hide almost everything on screen apart from the document

Launching Print Preview

Pull down the File menu and click Print Preview. This is the result:

Print Preview toolbar

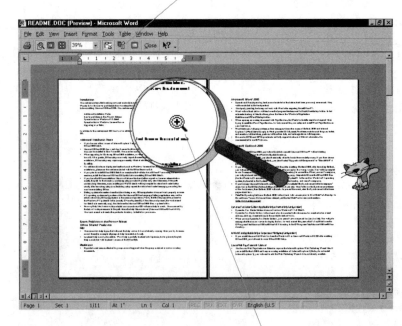

Magnifying cursor – see page 97

Zooming in or out in Print Preview

There are two ways in which you can change the display magnification in Print Preview mode.

Using the mouse

If you've just launched Print Preview, the Magnifier cursor will already be on-screen.

By default, the cursor in Print Preview is a magnifying glass – see the illustration on page 96 for what it looks like. You can use this to magnify *part* of the active document.

If the cursor currently isn't a magnifying glass, do the following in the Print Preview toolbar:

Click here

Now position the Magnifier cursor over the portion of the active document that you want to expand. Left-click once.

Using the Zoom Control button

To choose from pre-defined Zoom sizes, do the following:

Click here

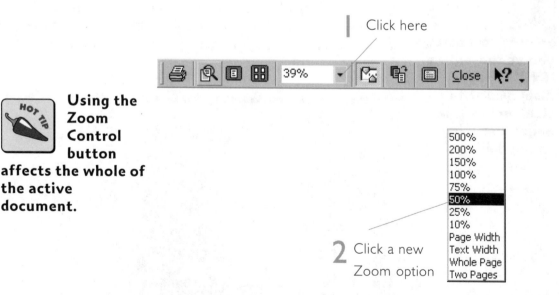

Using the Zoom Control button affects the whole of the active document.

2 Click a new Zoom option

Multiple pages in Print Preview

In Print Preview mode, you can view as many as thirty-two (4 x 8) pages at the same time.

Turn to the Print Preview toolbar and do the following:

Click here

Word launches a graphical list:

Click and hold here, then follow the instructions below

4 x 2 Pages

Word tells you here what page permutation you've chosen, e.g. '1 x 2' (2 pages displayed at full size), or '2 x 1' (2 pages displayed as thumbnails).

Position the mouse pointer over the first icon (see the illustration above). Hold down the left mouse button. Drag the pointer to the right and/or down (the list expands as you do so). When you find the right page multiple, release the mouse button.

4 x 2 view

Clearing the screen in Print Preview

We saw earlier that it's possible to hide superfluous screen components in Normal, Web Layout and Print Layout views. You can also do this in Print Preview mode. Word calls this Full Screen view.

The advantage is that using Full Screen view in Print Preview mode makes even more space available for display purposes. This is highly desirable unless you have a particularly large monitor. In Print Preview mode, Full Screen view hides all screen components with the exception of the Print Preview toolbar and the dedicated Full Screen toolbar.

Even the Office Assistant disappears off-screen.

Implementing Full Screen view

Refer to the Print Preview toolbar and do the following:

Click here

There are shortcuts you can use to leave Full Screen view:

- simply press Esc
- alternatively, click here:

To leave Full Screen view, repeat this procedure.

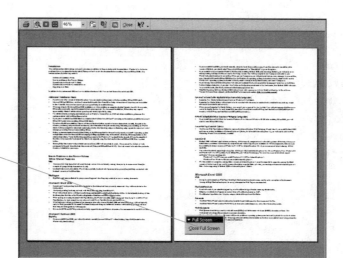

1 x 2 pages in Full Screen view

Printer setup

Most Word 2000 documents need to be printed eventually. Before you can begin printing, however, you need to ensure that:

The question of which printer you select affects how the document displays in Print Preview mode.

- the correct printer is selected (if you have more than one installed)

- the correct printer settings are in force

Word 2000 calls these collectively the 'printer setup'.

Irrespective of the printer selected, the settings vary in accordance with the job in hand. For example, most printer drivers (the software which 'drives' the printer) allow you to specify whether or not you want pictures printed. Additionally, they often allow you to specify the resolution or print quality of the output...

Selecting the printer and/or settings

At any time before you're ready to print a document, pull down the File menu and click Print. Now do the following:

Click here; select the printer you want from the list

This procedure can also be followed from within Print Preview mode.

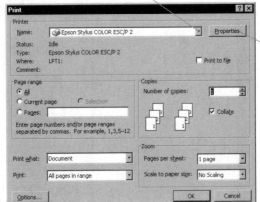

2 Click here to adjust printer settings (see your printer's manual for how to do this)

Now complete the remainder of the Print dialog, prior to printing your document (see pages 103–104).

Printing – an overview

Once the active document is how you want it (and you've customised the printer setup appropriately), you'll probably need to print it out. Word 2000 makes this process easy and straightforward. It lets you set a variety of options before you do so.

Alternatively, you can simply opt to print your document with the default options in force (Word 2000 provides a 'fast track' approach to this).

Available print options include:

- the number of copies you want printed

- whether you want the copies 'collated'. This is the process whereby Word 2000 prints one full copy at a time. For instance, if you're printing three copies of a 40-page document, Word prints pages 1–40 of the first document, followed by pages 1–40 of the second and pages 1–40 of the third

- which pages (or page ranges) you want printed

- whether you want to limit the print run to odd or even pages

- whether you want the print run restricted to text you selected before initiating printing

- whether you want the pages printed in reverse order (e.g. from the last page to the first)

- the quality of the eventual output (with many printers, Word 2000 allows you to print with minimal formatting for proofing purposes)

- whether you want to go on working in Word 2000 while the document prints (the default). Word 2000 calls this 'background printing'

You can 'mix and match' these, as appropriate.

Printing – the fast track approach

Since documents and printing needs vary dramatically, it's often necessary to customise print options before you begin printing.

For example, if you've created a document which contains numerous pictures, you may well want to print out a draft copy for proofing purposes prior to printing the final version (although Print Preview mode provides a very effective indication of how a document will look when printed, there are still errors which are only detectable when you're working with hard copy). In this situation, you may wish to exclude pictures or print with minimal formatting. (For how to set your own print options, see pages 103–104.)

On the other hand, simple documents can often benefit from a simple approach. In this case, you may well be content to print using the default options. Word 2000 recognises this and provides a method which bypasses the standard Print dialog, and is therefore much quicker and easier to use.

Printing with the current print options

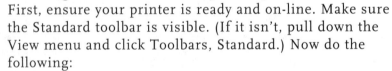

You can also access fast-track printing from within Print Preview.

Simply click this button:

in the Print Preview toolbar.

First, ensure your printer is ready and on-line. Make sure the Standard toolbar is visible. (If it isn't, pull down the View menu and click Toolbars, Standard.) Now do the following:

Click here

Word 2000 starts printing the active document immediately.

Customised printing

For more options, carry out the actions on page 104 before you perform step 5 here.

If you need to set revised print options before printing, do the following.

Pull down the File menu and click Print. Now carry out steps 1–5, as appropriate. Finally, carry out step 6.

To print only odd or even pages, click the Print field. Click Odd Pages or Even Pages.

1 Click here to deselect collation

2 Type in the number of copies

To print more than one page on a sheet, click Pages per sheet. Select a number in the list.

[Print dialog box]

Print

Printer
Name: Epson Stylus COLOR ESC/P 2   Properties
Status: Idle
Type: Epson Stylus COLOR ESC/P 2
Where: LPT1:
Comment:
Print to file

Page range
All
Current page
Pages:
Enter page numbers and/or page ranges separated by commas. For example, 1,3,5–12

Copies
Number of copies: 1
Collate

Print what: Document
Print: All pages in range

Zoom
Pages per sheet: 1 page
Scale to paper size: No Scaling

Options...   OK   Cancel

Re step 3 – separate non-adjacent pages with commas but no spaces – e.g. to print pages 5, 12, 16 and 19 type in:
5,12,16,19
** Enter contiguous pages with dashes – e.g. to print pages 12 to 23 inclusive, type in:**
12-23

3 Type in the relevant page range (see tip opposite)

4 Click here if you selected text before launching this dialog and this is all you want to print

5 Click here

Word starts printing the active document.

...cont'd

For further coverage of essential Word 2000 features, see 'Word 2000', also in the 'in easy steps' series.

Other print options are accessible from within a special dialog. This is launched from within the Print dialog.

First, pull down the File menu and click Print. Then do the following:

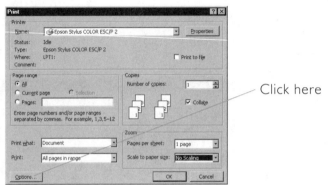

Click here

Re step 2 – if you want to speed up printing, deselect background printing. (But note that if you do this, you won't be able to continue working until printing is complete.)

Now perform steps 1–3 below, as appropriate. Then follow step 4.

1 Ensure this is selected to print with minimal formatting

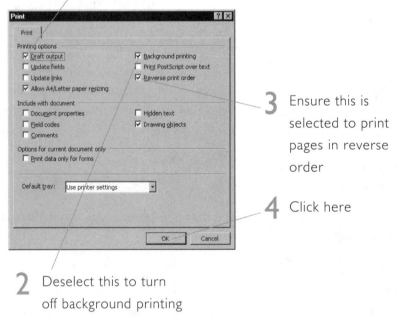

3 Ensure this is selected to print pages in reverse order

4 Click here

Step 4 returns you to the Print dialog. Now follow step 5 on page 103 to initiate printing.

2 Deselect this to turn off background printing

Excel 2000

Chapter Three

This chapter gives you the fundamentals of using Excel 2000 (including Year 2000 compliance). You'll work with data and formulas/functions, and move around through worksheets. Then you'll format your worksheets for maximum effect and search for specific data. You'll also insert pictures, and view your data graphically by converting it into a chart. Finally, you'll customise worksheet layout, preview your work and then print it.

Covers

The Excel 2000 screen

Below is a detailed illustration of the Excel 2000 screen.

Title bar   Menu bar   Column letters

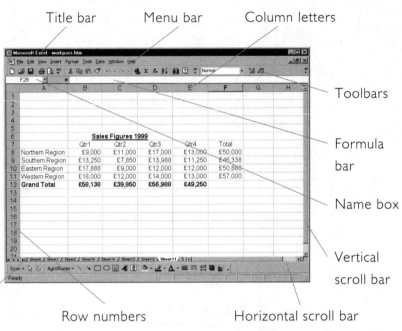

Toolbars

Formula bar

Name box

Vertical scroll bar

Row numbers   Horizontal scroll bar

This is the worksheet Tab area: The screen components here are used to move through Excel documents.

Some of these screen components can be hidden at will.

Specifying which screen components display

Pull down the Tools menu and click Options. Then:

Ensure the View tab is active

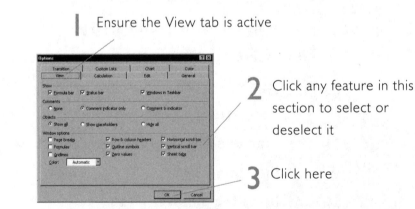

2 Click any feature in this section to select or deselect it

3 Click here

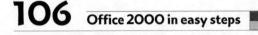

Entering data

When you start Excel 2000, you're presented with a new blank worksheet (spreadsheet):

When you run Excel 2000, you're actually opening a new workbook (see below). Excel calls these 'Book 1', 'Book 2' etc.

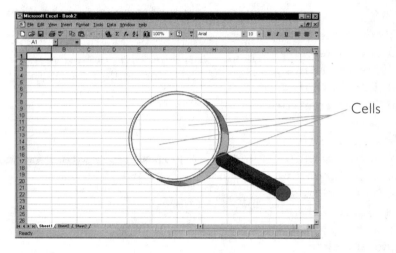

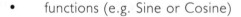

Cells

This means that you can start entering data immediately.

In Excel, you can enter the following basic data types:

- values (i.e. numbers)

- text (e.g. headings and explanatory material)

- functions (e.g. Sine or Cosine)

- formulas (combinations of values, text and functions)

Columns are vertical, rows horizontal. Each worksheet can have as many as 256 columns and 65,536 rows, making a grand total of 16,777,216 cells.

You enter data into 'cells'. Cells are formed where rows and columns intersect.

Collections of rows/columns and cells are known in Excel as worksheets. Worksheets are organised into workbooks (by default, each workbook has 3 worksheets). Workbooks are the files that are stored on disk when you save your work in Excel.

...cont'd

When you enter values which are too big (physically) to fit in the holding cell, Excel 2000 may insert an error message.
   To resolve this, widen the column (see the 'Amending row/column sizes' topic later). Or pull down the Format menu and click Column, Autofit Selection to have Excel automatically increase the column size to match the contents.

Although you can enter data *directly* into a cell (by simply clicking in the cell and typing it in), there's another method you can use which is often easier. Excel provides a special screen component known as the Formula bar.

The illustration below shows the end of a blank worksheet. Some sample text has been inserted into cell IV65536 (note that the Name box tells you which cell is currently active).

Name box

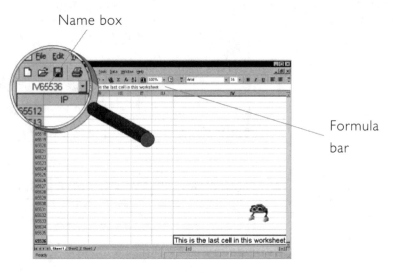

Formula bar

Entering data via the Formula bar
Click the cell you want to insert data into. Then click the Formula bar. Type in the data. Then follow step 1 below. If you decide not to proceed with the operation, follow step 2 instead:

You can use a keyboard route to confirm operations in the Formula bar: simply press Enter.

1 Click here

2 Click here

Modifying existing data

Re the tip below – remember, if you've used the Redo button before, Excel 2000 may have promoted it to the main body of the Standard toolbar.

You can amend the contents of a cell in two ways:

- via the Formula bar

- from within the cell

When you use either of these methods, Excel 2000 enters a special state known as Edit Mode.

Amending existing data using the Formula bar

Click the cell whose contents you want to change. Then click in the Formula bar. Make the appropriate revisions and/or additions. Then press Enter. Excel updates the relevant cell.

Amending existing data internally

Click the cell whose contents you want to change. Press F2. Make the appropriate revisions and/or additions *within the cell*. Then press Enter.

To redo an action, click ⏩ on the right of the Standard toolbar. In the flyout, do the following:

Click here

In the list, select a redo action but note that, if you select an early operation (i.e. one near the bottom), all later operations are included.

The illustration below shows a section from a simple workbook:

A magnified view of cell G15, in Edit Mode (note the flashing insertion point)

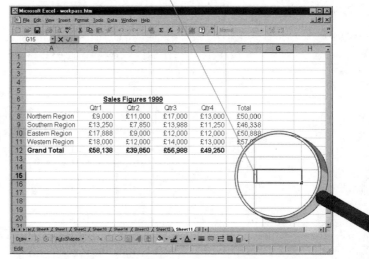

Working with cell ranges

When you're working with more than one cell, it's often convenient and useful to organise them in 'ranges'.

A range is a rectangular arrangement of cells. In the illustration below, cells A3, A4, A5, A6, B3, B4, B5 and B6 have been selected.

A selected cell range

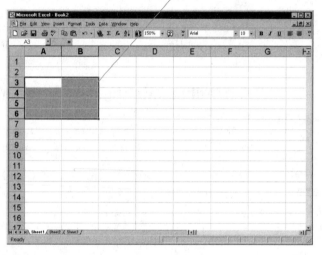

The above description of the relevant cells is very cumbersome. It's much more useful to use a form of shorthand. Excel 2000 (using the start and end cells as reference points) refers to these cells as:

A3:B6

You can extend this even more. Cell addresses can also incorporate a component which refers to the worksheet that contains the range. For example, to denote that the range A3:B6 is in a worksheet called Sheet8, you'd use:

Sheet8!A3:B6

Moving around in worksheets

Excel 2000 worksheets are huge. Moving to cells which happen to be visible is easy: you simply click in the relevant cell. However, Excel provides several techniques you can use to jump to less accessible areas.

Using the scroll bars

Use any of the following methods:

When you carry out step 1 on the right, Excel displays a bubble showing where you're up to:

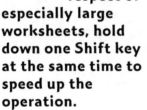

Row: 15

When you carry out step 1 in respect of especially large worksheets, hold down one Shift key at the same time to speed up the operation.

1. to scroll quickly to another section of the active worksheet, drag the scroll box along the scroll bar until you reach it

2. to move one window to the right or left, click to the left or right of the scroll box in the horizontal scroll bar

3. to move one window up or down, click above or below the scroll box in the vertical scroll bar

4. to move up or down by one row, click the arrows in the vertical scroll bar

5. to move left or right by one column, click the arrows in the horizontal scroll bar

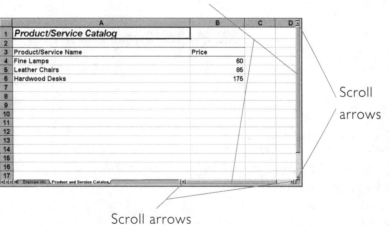

Scroll boxes

Scroll arrows

Scroll arrows

...cont'd

Excel 2000 facilitates worksheet navigation. As you move the insertion point from cell to cell, the relevant row and column headers are emboldened:

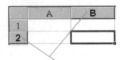

Illuminated headers

You can use a keyboard shortcut to launch this dialog. Simply press:
F5
or
Ctrl+G

Re step 1 - a cell's 'reference' (or 'address') identifies it in relation to its position in a worksheet, e.g. BII **or** H23. **You can also type in cell ranges here.**

Using the keyboard
You can use the following techniques:

1. use the cursor keys to move one cell left, right, up or down

2. hold down Ctrl as you use 1. above; this jumps to the edge of the current section (e.g. if cell BII is active and you hold down Ctrl as you press ➡, Excel jumps to IVII, the last cell in row II)

3. press Home to jump to the first cell in the active row, or Ctrl+Home to move to AI

4. press Page Up or Page Down to move up or down by one screen

5. press Alt+Page Down to move one screen to the right, or Alt+Page Up to move one screen to the left

Using the Go To dialog
Excel 2000 provides a special dialog which you can use to specify precise cell destinations.

Pull down the Edit menu and click Go To. Now do the following:

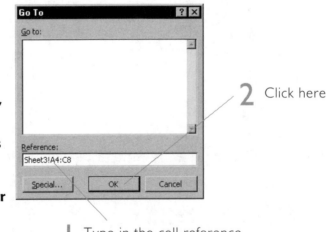

2 Click here

Type in the cell reference you want to move to

Switching between worksheets

Because workbooks have more than one worksheet, Excel provides two easy and convenient methods for moving between them.

See the lower DON'T FORGET icon on page 106 if you're not sure how to find the Tab area.

Using the Tab area
You can use the Tab area (at the base of the Excel screen) to:

- jump to the first or last sheet

- jump to the next or previous sheet

- jump to a specific sheet

See the illustration below:

To first sheet

To next sheet

Customised sheet tab

To previous sheet

To last sheet

Customised sheet tab

When you click a worksheet tab, Excel 2000 emboldens the name and makes the tab background white.

To move to a specific sheet, simply click the relevant tab.

An example: in the illustration above, to jump to the Customize Your Invoice worksheet, simply click the appropriate tab.

Using the keyboard
You can use keyboard shortcuts here:

Ctrl+Page Up   moves to the previous tab

Ctrl+Page Down   moves to the next tab

Viewing several worksheets

Excel 2000 also lets you view multiple worksheets simultaneously. This can be particularly useful when they have data in common. Viewing multiple worksheets is a two stage process:

A.   opening a new window

B.   selecting the additional worksheet

Opening a new window

Pull down the Window menu and do the following:

To switch between active windows, pull down the Window menu and click the relevant entry in the list at the bottom:

Window

| New Window |
| Arrange... |
| Hide |
| Unhide... |
| Split |
| Freeze Panes |
| 1 invoice1.xls |
| ✓ 2 Book2 |
| 3 usethis.xls |

Click here

Selecting the additional worksheet

Excel now launches a new window showing an alternative view of the active worksheet. Do the following:

If you want to work with alternative views of the *same* worksheet – a useful technique in itself – simply omit step 2.

	A	B	C	D	E	F	G	H	I
1									
2		Video Rentals				Rental			Net Profit
3						Price			Number of Ren
4		Rental Price=		£2.50		£400	100	125	150
5		Number of Rentals=		200		£1.00	£0.00	£25.00	£50.00
6		Total Income=		£500		£1.25	£25.00	£56.25	£87.50
7						£1.50	£50.00	£87.50	£125.00
8		Total Costs=		£100		£1.75	£75.00	£118.75	£162.50
9						£2.00	£100.00	£150.00	£200.00
10		Net Profit=		£400		£2.25	£125.00	£181.25	£237.50
11						£2.50	£150.00	£212.50	£275.00

2 Click the relevant sheet tab

Rearranging worksheet windows

When you have multiple worksheet windows open at once, you can have Excel arrange them in specific patterns. This is a useful technique because it makes worksheets more visible and accessible. Options are:

Use standard Windows techniques to move, close and resize open windows.

Tiled   Windows are displayed side by side:

Horizontal   Windows are displayed in a tiled column, with horizontal subdivisions:

Vertical   Windows are displayed in a tiled row, with vertical subdivisions:

Cascade   Windows are overlaid (with a slight offset):

Rearranging windows

Pull down the Window menu and click Arrange. Then:

1   Click an arrangement

2   Click here

Other operations on worksheets

We said earlier that, by default, each workbook has 3 worksheets. However, you can easily:

- add new worksheets

- delete existing worksheets

- move existing worksheets

Inserting a single worksheet
In the worksheet Tab area at the base of the screen, click the tab which represents the sheet in front of which you want the new worksheet inserted. Pull down the Insert menu and click Worksheet.

 You can use a keyboard shortcut to insert a worksheet. Simply press Shift+F11.

Inserting more than one worksheet
To add multiple worksheets, hold down one Shift key as you click the required number of sheet tabs (in other words, to add 6 new worksheets, shift-click 6 tabs). Then pull down the Insert menu and click Worksheet.

Deleting worksheets
In the worksheet Tab area, click a single worksheet tab (or shift-click multiple tabs to delete more than one worksheet at a time). Pull down the Edit menu and click Delete Sheet. Excel 2000 launches a special message. Do the following:

When you delete a worksheet, you automatically erase the worksheet contents, too.

Click here to proceed with the deletion

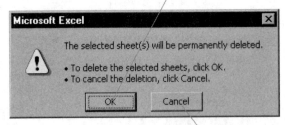

The selected sheet(s) will be permanently deleted.

- To delete the selected sheets, click OK.
- To cancel the deletion, click Cancel.

OK   Cancel

Or here to cancel it and return to your workbook

 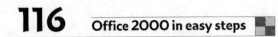

...cont'd

You can perform two kinds of move operation on worksheets. You can:

• rearrange the worksheet order within a given workbook

• transfer a worksheet to another workbook

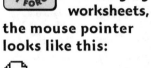

Rearranging worksheets

To select a single worksheet, click the relevant sheet tab in the worksheet Tab area. Or select more than one worksheet by holding down one Shift key as you click multiple tabs. With the mouse pointer still over the selected tab(s), hold down the left mouse button and drag them to their new location. Release the mouse button to confirm the operation.

Moving worksheets to another workbook

To select a single worksheet, click the relevant sheet tab in the worksheet Tab area. Or select more than one worksheet by holding down one Shift key as you click multiple tabs. Pull down the Edit menu and click Move or Copy Sheet. Now do the following:

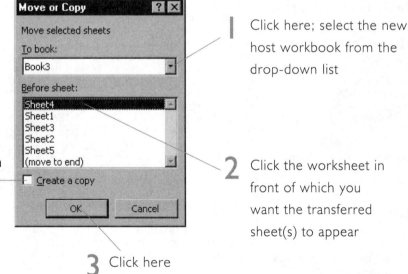

1 Click here; select the new host workbook from the drop-down list

2 Click the worksheet in front of which you want the transferred sheet(s) to appear

3 Click here

Selection techniques

Before you can carry out any editing operations on cells in Excel 2000, you have to select them first. Selecting a single cell is very easy: you merely click in it. However, Excel provides a variety of selection techniques which you can use to select more than one cell.

Selecting adjacent cell ranges

The easiest way to do this is to use the mouse. Click in the first cell in the range; hold down the left mouse button and drag over the remaining cells. Release the mouse button.

You can use the keyboard, too. Select the first cell in the range. Hold down one Shift key as you use the relevant cursor key to extend the selection. Release the keys when the correct selection has been defined.

Selecting separate cell ranges

Excel lets you select more than one range at a time. Look at the illustration below:

Shows that

Excel is in

Selection mode

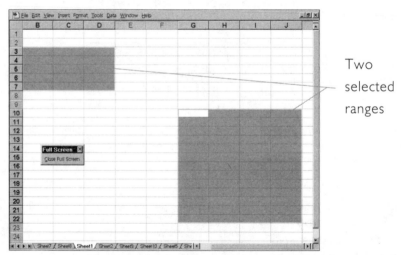

Two selected ranges

To select joint ranges, select the first in the normal way (you can only use the mouse method here). Then hold down Ctrl as you select subsequent ranges.

Selecting a single row or column

To select every cell within a row or column automatically, click the row or column heading.

Column heading

Row heading

Selecting multiple rows or columns

To select more than one row or column, click a row or column heading. Hold down the left mouse button and drag to select adjacent rows or columns.

Selecting an entire worksheet

Carry out step 1 below:

HOT TIP

You can use a keyboard shortcut to select every cell automatically. Simply press Ctrl+A.

HOT TIP

To undo the effect of step 1, simply click anywhere in the worksheet.

Click the Select All button

Formulas – an overview

Formulas are cell entries which define how other values relate to each other.

As a very simple example, consider the following:

The underlying formula – see below

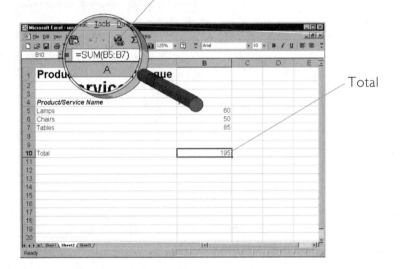

Total

Here, a cell has been defined which returns the total of cells B5:B7. Obviously, in this instance you could insert the total easily enough yourself because the individual values are so small, and because we're only dealing with a small number of cells. But what happens if the cell values are larger and/or more numerous, or – more to the point – if they're liable to change frequently?

The answer is to insert a formula which carries out the necessary calculation automatically.

If you look at the Formula bar in the illustration, you'll see the formula which does this:

=SUM(B5:B7)

Many Excel formulas are much more complex than this, but the principles remain the same.

Inserting a formula

Arguments (e.g. cell references) relating to functions are always contained in brackets.

All formulas in Excel 2000 begin with an equals sign. This is usually followed by a permutation of the following:

- an operand (cell reference, e.g. B4)

- a function (e.g. the summation function, SUM)

- an arithmetical operator (+, −, / and *)

- comparison operators (<, >, <=, >= and =)

Excel supports a very wide range of functions organised into numerous categories. For more information on how to insert functions, see page 122.

The mathematical operators are (in the order in which they appear in the list): *plus, minus, divide* and *multiply*.

To enter the same formula into a cell range, select the range, type the formula and then press Ctrl+Enter.

The comparison operators are (in the order in which they appear in the list): *less than, greater than, less than or equal to, greater than or equal to* and *equals*.

There are two ways to enter formulas:

Entering a formula directly into the cell

Click the cell in which you want to insert a formula. Then type = followed by your formula. When you've finished, press Enter.

Entering a formula into the Formula bar

This is usually the most convenient method.

Click the cell in which you want to insert a formula. Then click in the Formula bar. Type = followed by your formula. When you've finished, press Enter or do the following:

Click here

Inserting a function

Functions are pre-defined tools which accomplish specific tasks. These tasks are often calculations; occasionally, however, they're more generalised (e.g. some functions simply return dates and/or times). In effect, functions replace one or more formulas.

Excel 2000 provides a special dialog – the Formula Palette – to help ensure that you enter functions correctly. This is useful for the following reasons:

• Excel 2000 provides so many functions, it's convenient to apply them from a centralised source

• the Formula Palette ensures the functions are entered with the correct syntax

Functions can only be used in formulas.

Inserting a function with the Formula Palette

At the relevant juncture during the process of inserting a formula, refer to the Formula bar and do the following:

= ——— Click here

Now carry out the following steps:

Click here; select a function from the list

SUM	X ✓ = =SUM(B5:B7)

SUM
Number1 B5:B7   = {60;50;85}
Number2   = number

= 195

Adds all the numbers in a range of cells.

Number1: number1,number2,... are 1 to 30 numbers to sum. Logical values and text are ignored in cells, included if typed as arguments.

Formula result =195   OK   Cancel

2 Enter the function arguments

3 Click here

Amending row/column sizes

Sooner or later, you'll find it necessary to resize rows or columns. This necessity arises when there is too much data in cells to display adequately. You can enlarge or shrink single or multiple rows/columns.

Changing row height

To change one row's height, click the row heading. If you want to change multiple rows, hold down Ctrl and click the appropriate extra headings. Then place the mouse pointer (it changes to a cross) just under the row heading(s). Hold down the left mouse button and drag up or down to decrease or increase the row(s) respectively. Release the mouse button to confirm the operation.

Excel has a useful 'Best Fit' feature.
When the mouse pointer has changed to:

↕

double-click to have the row(s) or column(s) adjust themselves automatically to their contents.

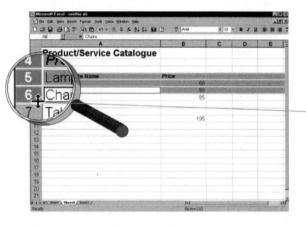

A magnified view of the transformed pointer – here, we're amending rows 4, 5 and 6 jointly

Changing column width

To change one column's width, click the column heading. If you want to change multiple columns, hold down Ctrl and click the appropriate extra headings. Then place the mouse pointer (it changes to a cross) just to the right of the column heading(s). Hold down the left mouse button and drag right or left to widen or narrow the column(s) respectively.

Release the mouse button to confirm the operation.

Inserting cells, rows or columns

You can insert additional cells, rows or columns into worksheets.

If you select cells in more than one row or column, Excel 2000 inserts the equivalent number of new rows or columns.

Inserting a new row or column

First, select one or more cells within the row(s) or column(s) where you want to carry out the insert operation. Now pull down the Insert menu and click Rows or Columns, as appropriate. Excel 2000 inserts the new row(s) or column(s) immediately.

	A	B	C
1	**Product/Service Catalogue**		
2			
3			
4	*Product/Service Name*	*Price*	
5	Lamps	60	
6	Chairs	50	
7	Tables	85	
8			
9			
10	Total	195	
11			
12			
13			
14			

Here, one new column or two new rows are being added

Inserting a new cell range

Select the range where you want to insert the new cells. Pull down the Insert menu and click Cells. Now carry out step 1 or step 2 below. Finally, follow step 3.

1 Click here to have Excel make room for the new cells by moving the selected range *to the right*

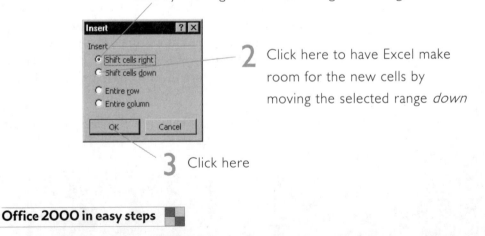

2 Click here to have Excel make room for the new cells by moving the selected range *down*

3 Click here

AutoFill

AutoFill extends formatting and formulas in lists.

Types of series you can use AutoFill to complete include:

- 1st Period, 2nd Period, 3rd Period etc.

- Mon, Tue, Wed etc.

- Quarter 1, Quarter 2, Quarter 3 etc.

- Week1, Week2, Week3 etc.

Data series don't need to contain every possibility. For instance, you could have:

- 1st Period, 3rd Period, 5th Period etc.

- Mon, Thu, Sun, Wed etc.

- Quarter 1, Quarter 4, Quarter 3, Quarter 2 etc.

- Week2, Week6, Week10, Week14 etc.

Excel 2000 lets you insert data series automatically. This is a very useful and timesaving feature. Look at the illustration below:

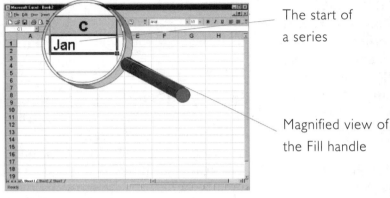

The start of a series

Magnified view of the Fill handle

If you wanted to insert month names in successive cells in column C, you could do so manually. But there's a much easier way. You can use Excel's AutoFill feature.

Using AutoFill to create a series

Type in the first element(s) of the series in consecutive cells. Select all the cells. Then position the mouse pointer over the Fill handle in the bottom right-hand corner of the last cell (the pointer changes to a crosshair). Hold down the left mouse button and drag the handle over the cells into which you want to extend the series (in the example above, over C2:C12). When you release the mouse button, Excel 2000 extrapolates the initial entry or entries into the appropriate series.

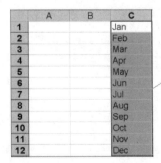

The completed series

Changing number formats

Excel 2000 lets you insert and work with Euros.

To insert the Euro symbol, hold down Alt and press the following on the Numerical keypad to the right of your keyboard:

0128

Finally, release the Alt key.

The only fonts which support the Euro are:

• Courier

• Tahoma

• Times

• Arial

Re step 3 – the options you can choose from vary according to the category chosen. Complete them as necessary.

Excel 2000 lets you apply formatting enhancements to cells and their contents. You can:

• specify a number format

• customise the font, type size and style of contents

• specify cell alignment

• border and/or shade cells

Specifying a number format

You can customise the way cell contents (e.g. numbers and dates/times) display in Excel. For example, you can specify at what point numbers are rounded up. Available formats are organised under several general categories. These include: Number, Accounting and Fraction.

Select the cells whose contents you want to customise. Pull down the Format menu and click Cells. Now do the following:

Ensure the Number tab is active

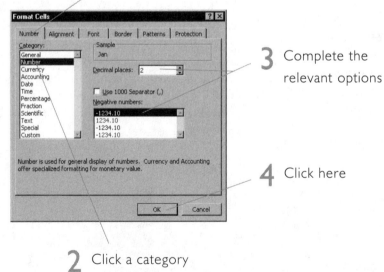

3 Complete the relevant options

4 Click here

2 Click a category

Changing fonts and styles

Excel supports Year 2000 date formats.
For instance:
12th December 2000 **appears (by default) as:**
12/12/00
(If you've specified a new date format in line with steps 2–3 on page 126, Excel may display it a little differently.)

Excel lets you carry out the following actions on cell contents (numbers and/or text). You can:

* apply a new font and/or type size

* apply a font style (for most fonts, you can choose from: Regular, Italic, Bold or Bold Italic)

* apply a colour

* apply a special effect: <u>underlining</u>, ~~strikethrough~~, superscript or subscript

Amending the appearance of cell contents

Select the cell(s) whose contents you want to reformat. Pull down the Format menu and click Cells. Carry out step 1 below. Now follow any of steps 2–5, as appropriate, or either or both of the HOT TIPS. Finally, carry out step 6.

To underline the specified contents, click the arrow to the right of the Underline box; select an underlining type in the list.

Ensure the Font tab is active

Format Cells

| Number | Alignment | Font | Border | Patterns | Protection |

Font:
Arial
- Aldus Palette Font
- Animals 1
- Animals 2
- Arial

Underline:
None

Effects
- Strikethrough
- Superscript
- Subscript

Font style:
Regular
- Regular
- Italic
- Bold
- Bold Italic

Color:
Automatic ☑ Normal font

Size:
10
- 8
- 9
- 10
- 11

Preview
AaBbCcYyZz

This is a TrueType font. The same font will be used on both your printer and your screen.

OK   Cancel

2 Type in a type size

5 Click the style you want to apply

6 Click here

To apply a special effect, click any of the options in the Effects section.

2 Click the font you want to use

4 Click here; click the colour you want to apply in the list

Cell alignment

By default, Excel 2000 aligns text to the left of cells, and numbers to the right. However, if you want you can change this.

You can specify alignment under two broad headings: Horizontal and Vertical.

Horizontal alignment

The main options are:

One further horizontal option – Center Across Selection – centres cell contents across more than one cell (if you selected a cell range before initiating it).

General	the default (see above)
Left	the contents are aligned from the left
Center	the contents are centred
Right	the contents are aligned from the right
Fill	the contents are duplicated so that they fill the cell
Justify	a combination of Left and Right

Vertical alignment

Available options are:

You can also rotate text within cells – see page 129 for more information.

Top	cell contents align with the top of the cell(s)
Center	the contents are centred
Bottom	the contents align with the cell bottom
Justify	the contents are aligned along the top and bottom of the cell(s)

Most of these settings parallel features found in Word 2000 (and many other word-processors). The difference, however, lies in the fact that Excel 2000 has to align data within the bounds of cells rather than a page. When it aligns text, it often needs to employ its own version of text wrap. See page 129 for more information on this.

Other alignment features you can set are rotation and text wrap.

Rotation controls the direction of text flow within cells; you achieve this by specifying a plus (anticlockwise) or minus (clockwise) angle.

When the Wrap Text option is selected, Excel – instead of overflowing any surplus text into adjacent cells to the right – forces it onto separate lines within the host cell.

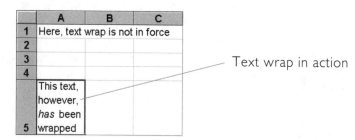

Text wrap in action

Customising cell alignment

Select the cell(s) whose contents you want to realign. Pull down the Format menu and click Cells. Carry out step 1 below. Follow steps 2–4, as appropriate. Finally, carry out step 5.

1 Ensure the Alignment tab is active

Select this to wrap text within the holding cell(s):

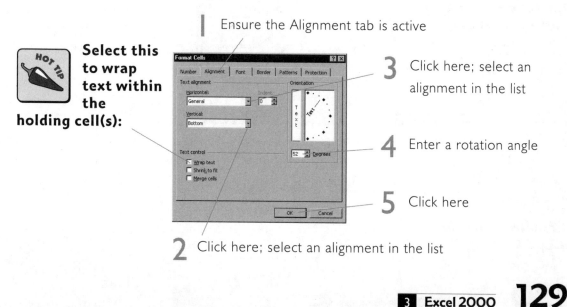

3 Click here; select an alignment in the list

4 Enter a rotation angle

5 Click here

2 Click here; select an alignment in the list

Bordering cells

Excel 2000 lets you define a border around:

- the perimeter of a selected cell range

- specific sides within a cell range

You can customise the border by choosing from a selection of pre-defined border styles. You can also add new line styles to specific sides, or colour the border.

Applying a cell border

First, select the cell range you want to border. Pull down the Format menu and click Cells. Now carry out step 1 below. Follow step 2 to apply an overall border. Carry out step 3 if you want to deactivate one or more border sides. Perform step 4 if you want to colour the border. Finally, carry out step 5:

If you want to customise the border style, click a line style here: immediately after step 2. Omit step 3. Follow step 4 if you want to colour the new style. Now do the following in this part of the dialog:

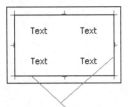

Click any of the 4 borders to apply the new style

Finally, carry out step 5.

| Ensure the Border tab is active

2 Click the relevant border style option

4 Optional – click here and select a colour in the list

5 Click here

3 Optional – click any border option in this section to deselect it

Shading cells

Excel 2000 lets you apply the following to cells:

You can only apply a foreground colour if you also apply a foreground pattern.

- a background colour
- a foreground pattern
- a foreground colour

Interesting effects can be achieved by using pattern and colour combinations with coloured backgrounds.

Applying a pattern or background

First, select the cell range you want to shade. Pull down the Format menu and click Cells. Now carry out step 1. Perform step 2 to apply a *background* colour, and/or 3–5 to apply a *foreground* pattern or a pattern/colour combination. Finally, follow step 6.

| Ensure the Patterns tab is active

The Sample field previews how your background and pattern/colour will look.

Step 5 is only effective if you've also carried out step 4.

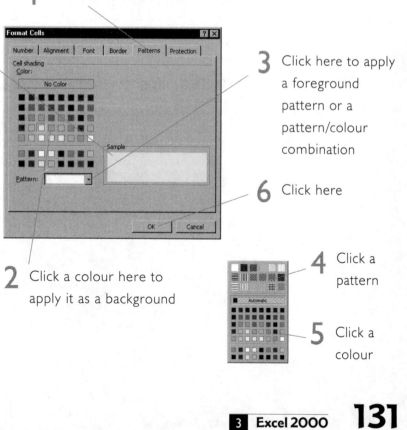

3 Click here to apply a foreground pattern or a pattern/colour combination

6 Click here

2 Click a colour here to apply it as a background

4 Click a pattern

5 Click a colour

AutoFormat

Excel 2000 provides a shortcut to the formatting of worksheet data: AutoFormat.

AutoFormat consists of 16 pre-defined formatting schemes. These incorporate specific excerpts from the font, number, alignment, border and shading options discussed earlier. You can apply any of these schemes (and their associated formatting) to selected cell ranges with just a few mouse clicks. You can even specify which scheme elements you *don't* wish to use.

AutoFormat works with most arrangements of worksheet data.

Using AutoFormat

First, select the cell range you want to apply an automatic format to. Pull down the Format menu and click AutoFormat. Now carry out step 1 below. Steps 2–3 are optional. Finally, follow step 4:

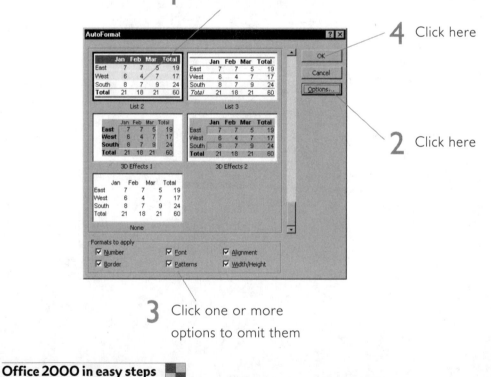

1 Select an AutoFormat

4 Click here

2 Click here

3 Click one or more options to omit them

The Format Painter

Re. step 1 – double-click the Format Painter icon if you want to apply the selected formatting more than once. Then repeat step 2 as often as necessary.
   Press Esc when you've finished.

Excel 2000 provides a very useful tool which can save you a lot of time and effort: the Format Painter. You can use the Format Painter to copy the formatting attributes from cells you've previously formatted to other cells, in one operation.

Using the Format Painter

First, apply the necessary formatting, if you haven't already done so. Then select the formatted cells. Click ❯ in the Standard toolbar, then do the following:

Click the Format Painter icon

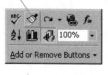

Re step 1 – if you've used the Format Painter button before, Excel 2000 may have promoted it to the main body of the Standard toolbar.

Pre-formatted text

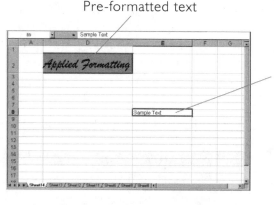

2 Select the cell(s) you want the formatting copied to

When you've finished using the Format Painter (or before, if you decide you don't want to proceed), press Esc.

The end result

Find operations

Excel 2000 lets you search for and jump to text or numbers (in short, any information) in your worksheets. This is a particularly useful feature when worksheets become large and complex.

You can organise your search by rows or by columns. You can also specify whether Excel looks in:

- cells that contain formulas

- cells that don't contain formulas

Additionally, you can insist that Excel only flag exact matches (i.e. if you searched for 11, Excel would not find 1111), and you can also limit text searches to text which has the case you specified (e.g. searching for PRODUCT LIST would not find Product List or product list).

Searching for data

Place the mouse pointer at the location in the active worksheet from which you want the search to begin. Pull down the Edit menu and click Find. Now carry out step 1 below, then any of steps 2–5. Finally, carry out step 6.

To search for data over more than one worksheet, select the relevant sheet tabs before launching the Find dialog.

If you want to restrict the search to specific cells, select a cell range *before* you launch the Find dialog.

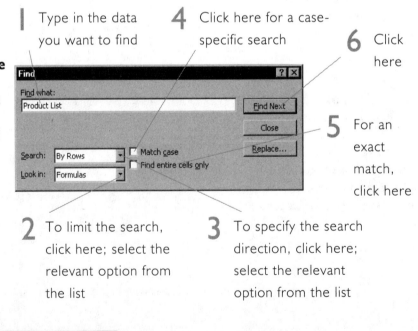

1 Type in the data you want to find

4 Click here for a case-specific search

6 Click here

5 For an exact match, click here

2 To limit the search, click here; select the relevant option from the list

3 To specify the search direction, click here; select the relevant option from the list

Find-and-replace operations

To replace data over more than one worksheet, select the relevant sheet tabs before launching the Replace dialog.

When you search for data, you can also – if you want – have Excel 2000 replace it with something else.

Find-and-replace operations can be organised by rows or columns. However, unlike straight searches, you can't specify whether Excel looks in cells that contain formulas or not. As with straight searches, you can, however, limit find-and-replace operations to exact matches and also (in the case of text) to precise case matches.

Normally, find-and-replace operations only affect the host worksheet. If you want to carry out an operation over multiple worksheets, see the HOT TIP.

If, when you carry out step 4, Excel finds an instance of the search text you *don't* want replaced, simply repeat step 3 instead.

Running a find-and-replace operation

Place the mouse pointer at the location in the active worksheet from which you want the search to begin (or select a cell range if you want to restrict the find-and-replace operation to this). Pull down the Edit menu and click Replace. Now carry out steps 1–3 below. Finally, carry out step 4 as often as required, or perform step 5 once for a global substitution.

Between steps 2-3, you can also elect to do any of the following:

- Click 'Match case' for a case-specific text search
- Click 'Find entire cells only' for an exact match
- Click in the 'Search' field to specify a search direction – select an option in the drop-down list

1 Type in the data you want to find

3 Click here to find the 1st occurrence

4 Click here to replace it

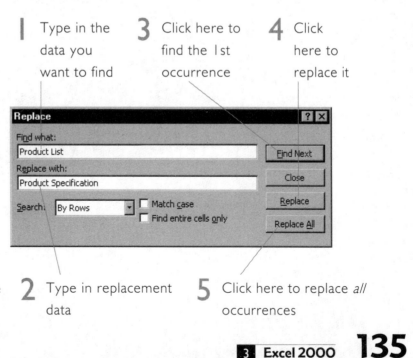

2 Type in replacement data

5 Click here to replace *all* occurrences

Charting – an overview

Excel 2000 has comprehensive charting capabilities. You can have it convert selected data into its visual equivalent. To do this, Excel offers a wide number of chart formats and sub-formats.

You can add a picture to chart walls:

Select the wall(s) in the normal way. Then follow the procedures set out on page 140.

You can create a chart:

- as a picture within the parent worksheet

- as a separate chart sheet

Chart sheets have their own tabs in the Tab area; these operate just like worksheet tabs.

Excel uses a special Wizard – the Chart Wizard – to make the process of creating charts as easy and convenient as possible.

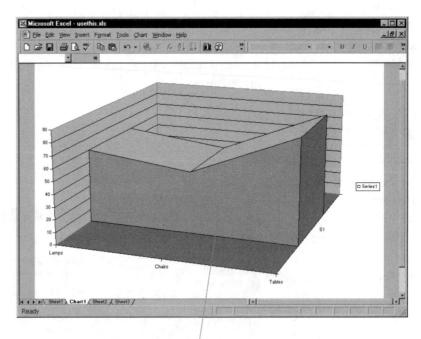

A 3-D Area chart

Creating a chart

First, select the cells you want converted into a chart. Pull down the Insert menu and click Chart. The first Chart Wizard dialog appears. Do the following:

1 Click a chart type

Click and hold here: to have Excel preview the selected chart combination in the Chart sub-type field.

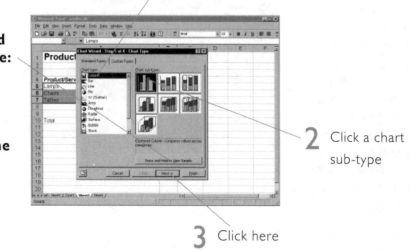

2 Click a chart sub-type

3 Click here

Re step 4 – click the Collapse Dialog button:

to hide the dialog temporarily while you select an alternative cell range. When you've finished, do the following:

There are three more dialogs to complete. Carry out the following steps:

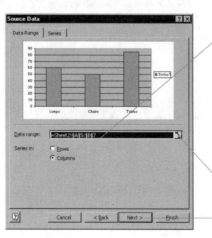

4 If you selected the wrong cells before launching the Chart Wizard, click here; then carry out the procedures in the HOT TIP

The Collapse Dialog button

5 Click here

Click here

Click any of the additional tabs to set further chart options.
For example, activate the Gridlines tab to specify how and where gridlines display. Or click Legend to determine where legends (text labels) display...

Excel 2000 now launches the third Chart Wizard dialog. Carry out the following additional steps:

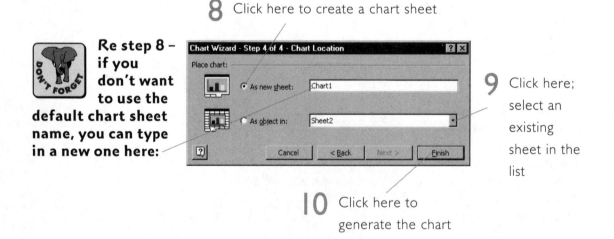

6 Optional – name the chart and/or axes

7 Click here

In the final dialog, you tell Excel whether you want the chart inserted into the current worksheet, or into a new chart sheet.

Carry out step 8 OR 9 below. Finally, perform step 10.

8 Click here to create a chart sheet

Re step 8 – if you don't want to use the default chart sheet name, you can type in a new one here:

9 Click here; select an existing sheet in the list

10 Click here to generate the chart

Inserting pictures

You can insert pictures into worksheets in two ways:

* with the Office Clip Gallery

* using a separate dialog

All clips have associated keywords. You can use these to locate clips.
Click in this field in the Gallery:

Type one or more words...	▾

Now type in one or more keywords. Finally, press Enter – any relevant clips display.

Re step 2 – the Clip Gallery organises clips under overall categories.

To see more Gallery clips, click this:

Keep Looking

Inserting pictures via the Clip Gallery

First, position the insertion point at the location within the active worksheet where you want to insert the picture. Pull down the Insert menu and click Picture, Clip Art. Do the following:

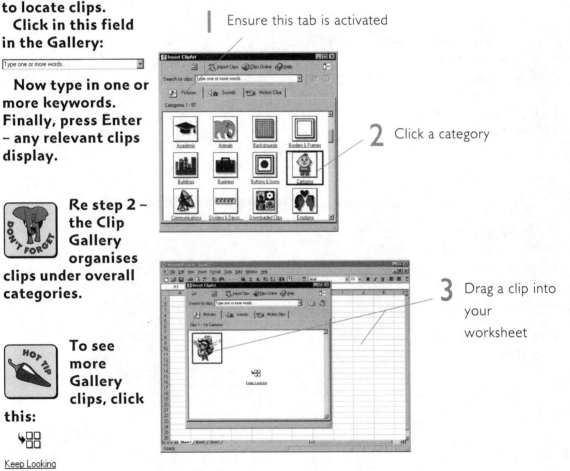

Ensure this tab is activated

2 Click a category

3 Drag a clip into your worksheet

4 Release the mouse button – Excel 2000 inserts the picture

...cont'd

Once inserted into a worksheet, pictures can be resized and moved in the normal way – see pages 89–92 for guidelines.

You can also insert pictures onto chart walls – see the HOT TIP on page 136.

Excel 2000 provides a preview of what the picture will look like when it's been imported. (See the Preview box on the right of the dialog.)

Inserting pictures – the dialog route

First, position the insertion point at the location within the active worksheet where you want to insert the picture. Pull down the Insert menu and do the following:

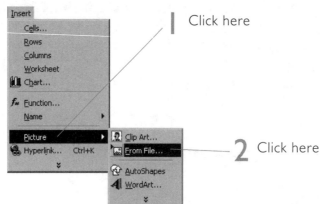

1 Click here

2 Click here

4 Click here. In the drop-down list, click the drive/folder that hosts the picture

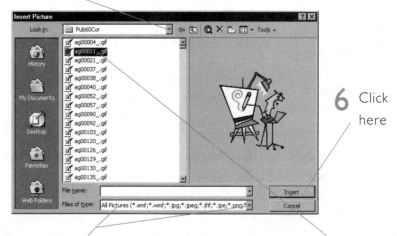

6 Click here

3 Make sure All Pictures... is showing. If it isn't, click the arrow and select it from the drop-down list

5 Click a picture file

Page setup – an overview

Excel 2000 has a special view mode – Page Break Preview – which you can also use to ensure your worksheet prints correctly.
Pull down the View menu and click Page Break Preview. Do the following (the white area denotes cells which will print, the grey those which won't):

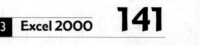

Drag page break margins to customise the printable area

(To leave Page Break Preview when you've finished with it, click Normal in the View menu.)

Making sure your worksheets print with the correct page setup can be a complex issue, for the simple reason that most worksheets become very extensive with the passage of time (so large, in fact, that in the normal course of things they won't fit onto a single page).

Page setup features you can customise include:

- the paper size and orientation
- scaling
- the starting page number
- the print quality
- margins
- header/footer information
- page order
- which worksheet components print

Margin settings you can amend are:

- top
- bottom
- left
- right

Additionally, you can set the distance between the top page edge and the top of the header, and the distance between the bottom page edge and the bottom edge of the footer.

When you save your active workbook, all Page Setup settings are saved with it.

Setting page options

 Charts in separate chart sheets have unique page setup options – see page 146.

Excel 2000 comes with 17 pre-defined paper sizes which you can apply to your worksheets, in either portrait (top-to-bottom) or landscape (sideways on) orientation. This is one approach to effective printing. Another is scaling: you can print out your worksheets as they are, or you can have Excel shrink them so that they fit a given paper size (you can even automate this process). Additionally, you can set the print resolution and starting page number.

Using the Page tab in the Page Setup dialog

Pull down the File menu and click Page Setup. Now carry out step 1 below, followed by steps 2–6 as appropriate. Finally, carry out step 7:

Re step 5 – by default, Excel numbers pages from '1'. Leave the First page number field setting as Auto if you want this.

1 Ensure the Page tab is active

2 Click the orientation you need

3 Click here; click the page size you need in the drop-down list

To make your worksheet print in a specific number of pages, complete the 'Fit to' fields.

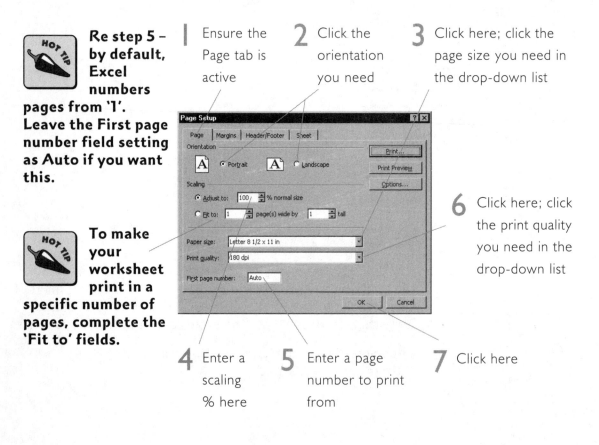

6 Click here; click the print quality you need in the drop-down list

4 Enter a scaling % here

5 Enter a page number to print from

7 Click here

Setting margin options

Excel 2000 lets you set a variety of margin settings. The illustration below shows the main ones:

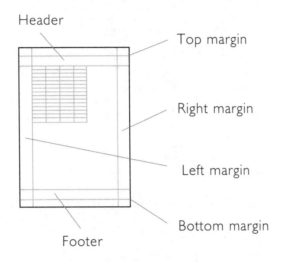

Header

Top margin

Right margin

Left margin

Bottom margin

Footer

Using the Margins tab in the Page Setup dialog

Pull down the File menu and click Page Setup. Now carry out step 1 below, followed by steps 2–3 as appropriate. Finally, carry out step 4:

1 Ensure the Margins tab is active

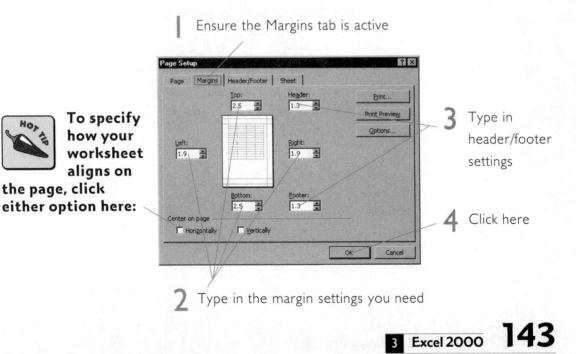

To specify how your worksheet aligns on the page, click either option here:

3 Type in header/footer settings

4 Click here

2 Type in the margin settings you need

Setting header/footer options

Excel 2000 provides a list of built-in header and footer settings. You can apply any of these to the active worksheet. These settings include:

You can also use specific groups of these e.g.:

- Page 1, Book 1
- Confidential, Sheet 1, Page 1

- the worksheet title

- the workbook title

- the page number

- the user's name

- 'Confidential'

- the date

Using the Header/Footer tab in the Page Setup dialog

Pull down the File menu and click Page Setup. Now carry out step 1 below, followed by steps 2–3 as appropriate. Finally, carry out step 4:

1 Ensure the Header/Footer tab is active

2 Click here; select a header from the list

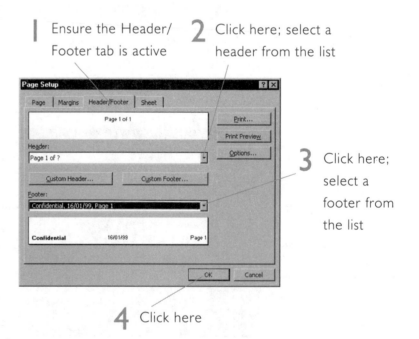

3 Click here; select a footer from the list

4 Click here

Setting sheet options

Excel 2000 lets you:

- define a printable area on-screen

- define a column or row title which will print on every page

- specify which worksheet components should print

- print with minimal formatting

- determine the print direction

Using the Sheet tab in the Page Setup dialog

Pull down the File menu and click Page Setup. Now carry out step 1 below, followed by steps 2–4 (and the tips) as appropriate. Finally, carry out step 5.

If you want to print a specific cell range (print area), type in the address here:

Click Draft Quality for rapid printing with the minimum of formatting.

Ensure the Sheet tab is active

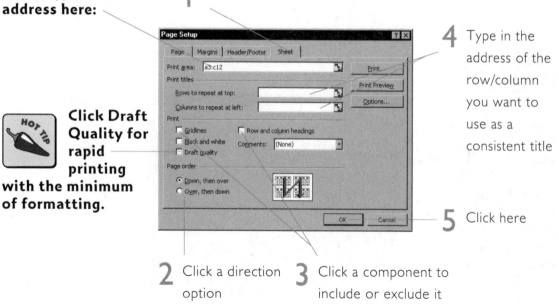

4 Type in the address of the row/column you want to use as a consistent title

5 Click here

2 Click a direction option

3 Click a component to include or exclude it

Page setup for charts

Most page setup issues for charts in chart sheets are identical to those for worksheet data. The main difference, however, is that the Page Setup dialog has a Chart (rather than a Sheet) tab.

In the Chart tab, you can opt to have the chart

- printed at full size

- scaled to fit the page

- user-defined

You can also set the print quality.

Using the Chart tab in the Page Setup dialog

Click the relevant chart tab in the worksheet Tab area. Pull down the File menu and click Page Setup. Now carry out step 1 below, followed by steps 2–3 as appropriate. Finally, carry out step 4.

Re step 3 – clicking Custom ensures that, when you return to the chart sheet, the chart size can be adjusted with the mouse in the normal way. The chart then prints at whatever size you set.

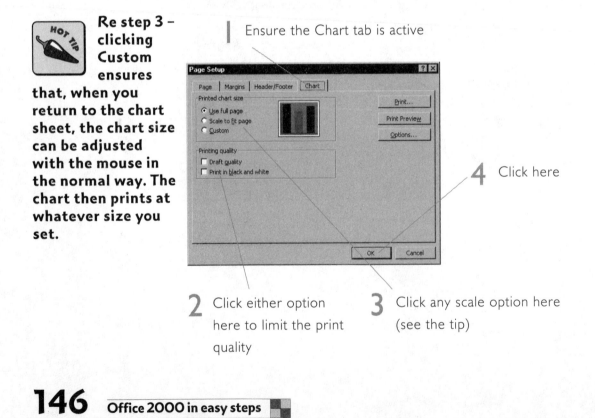

Ensure the Chart tab is active

4 Click here

2 Click either option here to limit the print quality

3 Click any scale option here (see the tip)

Launching Print Preview

Print Preview displays data in greyscale (rather than colour).

Excel 2000 provides a special view mode called Print Preview. This displays the active worksheet as it will look when printed. Use Print Preview as a final check just before you begin printing.

You can perform the following actions from within Print Preview:

Excel's Print Preview mode has only two Zoom settings:

• Full Page

• High-Magnification

- moving from page to page

- zooming in or out on the active page

- adjusting most Page Setup settings

- adjusting margins visually

Launching Print Preview

Pull down the File menu and click Print Preview. This is the result:

Special Print Preview toolbar

To leave Print Preview mode and return to your worksheet (or chart sheet), simply press Esc.

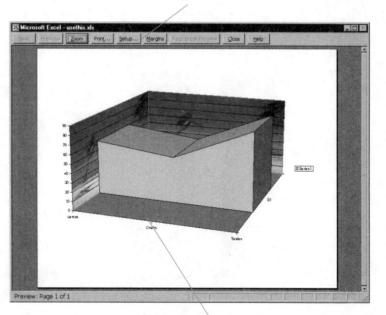

A preview of a chart sheet

Working with Print Preview

All of the operations you can perform in Print Preview mode can be accessed via the toolbar.

Click the Page Break Preview button to launch this view – see page 141 for how to use it.

Using the Print Preview toolbar

Do any of the following, as appropriate:

Re step 6 – see earlier topics (pages 141–146) for how to use the Page Setup dialog.

1 Click here to jump to the next page

3 Click here to zoom in or out

6 Click here to launch the Page Setup dialog

| Next | Previous | Zoom | Print... | Setup... | Margins | Page Break Preview | Close | Help |

2 Click here to jump to the previous page

4 Click here to toggle margin markers on or off – then follow step 5

5 Drag any margin to reposition it

Magnified view of Move pointer

Printing worksheet data

Excel 2000 lets you specify:

- the number of copies you want printed

- whether you want the copies 'collated'. This is the process whereby Excel prints one full copy at a time. For instance, if you're printing three copies of a 10-page worksheet, Excel prints pages 1–10 of the first copy, followed by pages 1–10 of the second and pages 1–10 of the third.

- which pages (or page ranges) you want printed

- whether you want the print run restricted to cells you selected before initiating printing

You can 'mix and match' these, as appropriate.

To select and print more than one worksheet, hold down Shift as you click on multiple tabs in the worksheet Tab area.

Starting a print run

Open the workbook that contains the data you want to print. If you want to print an entire worksheet, click the relevant tab in the worksheet Tab area. If you need to print a specific cell range within a worksheet, select it. Then pull down the File menu and click Print. Do any of steps 1–5. Then carry out step 6 to begin printing.

To adjust your printer's internal settings before you initiate printing, click Properties: Then refer to your printer's manual.

Click here; select the printer you want from the list

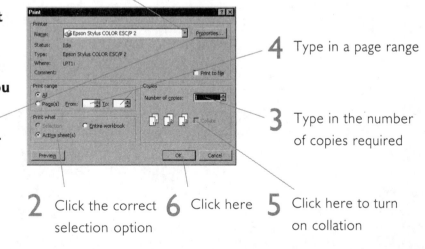

4 Type in a page range

3 Type in the number of copies required

2 Click the correct selection option

6 Click here

5 Click here to turn on collation

Printing – the fast track approach

In earlier topics, we looked at how to customise print options to meet varying needs and worksheet sizes. However, Excel 2000 – like Word 2000 – recognises that there will be times when you won't need this level of complexity. There are occasions when you'll merely want to print out your work – often for proofing purposes – with the standard print defaults applying, and with the absolute minimum of mouse actions.

For this reason, Excel provides a method which bypasses the standard Print dialog, and is therefore much quicker and easier to use.

For further coverage of essential Excel 2000 features, see 'Excel 2000', also in the 'in easy steps' series.

The default print options are:

- Excel prints only the active worksheet

- Excel prints only 1 copy

- Excel prints all pages within the active worksheet

- collation is turned off

Printing with the default print options

First, click the tab that relates to the worksheet you want to print. Ensure your printer is ready. Make sure the Standard toolbar is visible. (If it isn't, pull down the View menu and click Toolbars, Standard.) Now do the following:

Click here

Excel 2000 starts printing the active worksheet immediately, using the defaults listed above.

PowerPoint 2000

Chapter Four

This chapter gives you the fundamentals of producing your own slide show. You'll use the AutoContent Wizard to automate the creation of a presentation, and then customise it for your own use. You'll add/format text; work with slide views; insert pictures and hyperlinks; and apply new colour schemes. Finally, you'll print out your presentation and run it – in PowerPoint 2000, Internet Explorer and on machines which have neither installed.

Covers

The PowerPoint 2000 screen

Below is a detailed illustration of the PowerPoint 2000 screen.

Outline view only shows the textual components of slides.

Clicking a slide's entry displays it in the Slide area.

You can enter speaker notes into Notes view.

Click in Notes view. Type in the relevant text. When you've finished, click back in the Slide area.

Title bar   Menu bar   Rulers

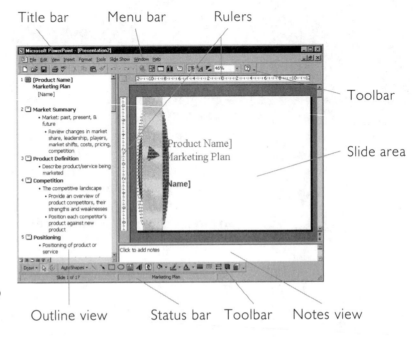

Toolbar

Slide area

Outline view   Status bar   Toolbar   Notes view

Some of these components can be hidden, if required.

Specifying which screen components display

Pull down the Tools menu and click Options. Then:

1 | Ensure the View tab is active

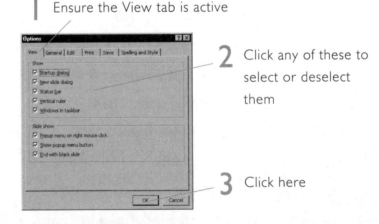

2 Click any of these to select or deselect them

3 Click here

The AutoContent Wizard

You can also launch the Wizard when you start PowerPoint. Do the following:

In chapter 1, we looked at how to create new Office documents based on templates and Wizards. PowerPoint 2000 has a unique and particularly detailed Wizard which handles the basics of creating a presentation.

Creating a new presentation with the AutoContent Wizard

Pull down the File menu and click New. Now do the following:

A Click here

B Click here

Now complete the AutoContent Wizard dialogs.

| Ensure this tab is active

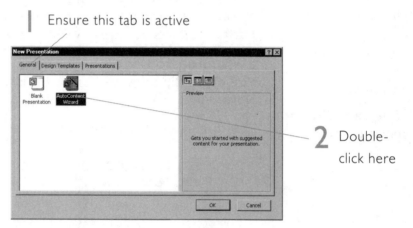

2 Double-click here

PowerPoint now launches the Wizard. Do the following:

The Wizard produces a 'standard' slide show which you can amend later, if you want.

3 Click here

See Chapter 1 for how to create a blank presentation, or a slide show based on a template.

Complete the remaining four dialogs in the normal way. In the final AutoContent dialog, click Finish to have PowerPoint generate the presentation.

The slide views – an overview

Normal view also includes the following:

- *Outline view* – shows the textual structure underlying slides
- *Notes view* – shows the speaker notes associated with the active slide

See page 152 for a visual description.

PowerPoint has the following views:

Normal	displays each slide individually
Slide Sorter	shows all the slides as icons, so you can manipulate them more easily
Notes Page	shows each slide together with any speaker notes

These are different ways of looking at your slide show. Normal view provides a very useful overview, while Slide Sorter view lets you modify more than one slide at a time.

Switching to a view

Pull down the View menu and click Normal, Slide Sorter or Notes Page.

The three views are compared below:

Normal view

Slide Sorter view

Notes Page view

Using the slide views

All the views have their own default magnification. You can adjust this, however.

Pull down the View menu and click Zoom. Do the following:

A Click a Zoom %

B Click here

You can also use Slide Sorter view to perform additional operations – for instance, you can use it to apply a new slide layout (see page 156) to more than one slide at a time.

The following are some brief supplementary notes on how best to use the PowerPoint 2000 views.

Normal view

Normal view displays the current slide in its own window. Use Normal view when you want a detailed picture of a slide (for instance, when you amend any of the slide contents, or when you change the overall formatting).

You can also use Normal view to:

- work with text. The Outline view component – see page 152 – displays only text. You can amend this and watch your changes take effect in the Slide area on the right

- enter notes. Simply click in the Notes view below the Slide area and enter speaker note text. (You can also do this within Notes Page view – see below)

To switch from slide to slide, you can press Page Up or Page Down as appropriate. (For more information on how to move around in presentations, see 'Moving through presentations' on page 162.)

Slide Sorter view

If you need to rearrange the order of slides, use Slide Sorter view. You can simply click on a slide and drag it to a new location (to move more than one slide, hold down one Ctrl key as you click them, then release the key and drag). You can also copy a slide by holding down Ctrl *as you drag*.

Notes Page view

This view is an aid to the presenter rather than the viewer of the slide show. If you want to enter speaker notes on a slide (for later printing), use Notes Page view.

In Notes Page view, the slide is displayed at a reduced size at the top of the page. Below this is a standard PowerPoint 2000 text object. For how to enter notes in this, see the 'Adding text to slides' topic on page 157.

Customising slide structure

The easiest way to customise the basic format of a slide is to use AutoLayout. AutoLayout offers a selection of 24 layout structures and lets you apply your choice to a specific slide or group of slides. When you've done this, you can then amend the individual components (see later topics).

You can select more than one slide in Slide Sorter view by holding down Ctrl as you click on the slide icons.

Using AutoLayout

Make sure you're in Slide or Slide Sorter view. If you're in Slide Sorter view, click the slide(s) you want to amend. Pull down the Format menu and click Slide Layout. Then do the following:

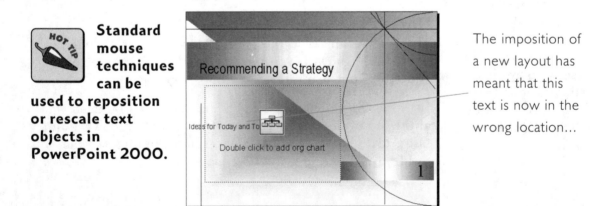

Click a slide layout

2 Click here

Any slide components present before you applied the new format will still remain. However, they may need to be resized or moved. Look at the illustration below:

Standard mouse techniques can be used to reposition or rescale text objects in PowerPoint 2000.

The imposition of a new layout has meant that this text is now in the wrong location...

Adding text to slides

To create a blank slide show, click New in the File menu. Click the General tab in the New Presentation dialog. Now double-click the Blank Presentation icon.
 Or, to create a blank slide show when you start PowerPoint 2000, click Blank presentation in the launch dialog. Click OK.

When you create a new slide show (unless you choose to create a blank presentation), PowerPoint 2000 fills each slide with placeholders containing sample text. The idea is that you should replace this with your own text.

The illustration below shows a sample slide before customisation:

Text placeholders

To insert your own text, click in any text placeholder. PowerPoint displays a text entry box. Now do the following:

When you type in text, certain errors are automatically corrected e.g.:

- the first letter in sentences is capitalised
- day names are capitalised
- specific errors are corrected (e.g. 'abbout' becomes 'about')

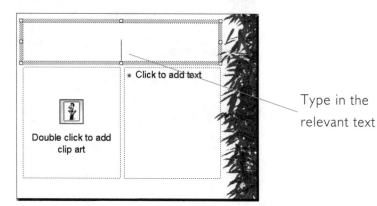

Type in the relevant text

Finally, click anywhere outside the placeholder to confirm the addition of the new text.

Formatting text

You can format text in a variety of ways. You can:

- change the font and/or type size

- apply a font style or effect

- apply a colour

- specify the alignment

- specify the line spacing

**Re step 6 –
if none of
the colours
here are
suitable, click More
Colors. In the Colors
dialog, ensure the
Standard tab is
active. Click a
colour in the
polygon in the
centre. Then click
OK. Finally, follow
step 7.**

Font-based formatting

Click inside the relevant text object and select the text you
want to format. Pull down the Format menu and click Font.
Now carry out any of steps 1–4 below, as appropriate. If you
want to re-colour the text, carry out steps 5–6. Finally,
follow step 7:

1 Click a new typeface

2 Type in a new point size

7 Click here

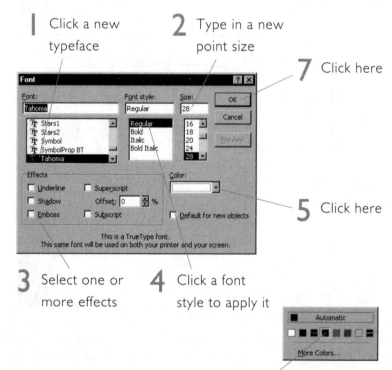

5 Click here

3 Select one or more effects

4 Click a font style to apply it

6 Click a colour (see the tip)

You can summarise specific slides.

When you do this, PowerPoint 2000 collects the slide titles and inserts them into a new slide.

In Slide Sorter view, select the relevant slides (they must contain titles). Then click the Summary Slide button:

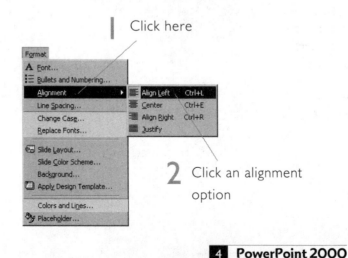

in the Slide Sorter toolbar. The new slide is inserted in front of the first selected slide.

Changing text spacing

First, click inside the relevant text object and select the text whose spacing you want to amend. Pull down the Format menu and click Line Spacing. Now carry out any of steps 1–3 below, as appropriate. Then follow step 4.

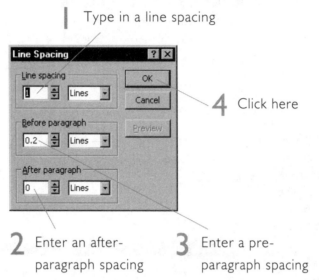

1 Type in a line spacing

4 Click here

2 Enter an after-paragraph spacing

3 Enter a pre-paragraph spacing

Changing text alignment

First, click inside the relevant text object and select the text whose alignment you want to amend. Pull down the Format menu and do the following:

1 Click here

2 Click an alignment option

Applying colour schemes

Applying a new colour scheme is a quick and effective way to give a presentation a new and consistent look.

Any PowerPoint 2000 presentation (apart from a blank one) automatically has various colour schemes available to it.

Imposing a colour scheme

If you want to restrict the colour scheme to one or more slides, first do one of the following:

- In Normal view, go to the slide whose colour scheme you want to replace

- In Slide Sorter view, select one or more slides

 Click the Preview button on the right to see what your slide(s) would look like after the application of the colour scheme.

Now pull down the Format menu and click Slide Color Scheme. Now carry out the following additional actions:

Ensure this tab is active

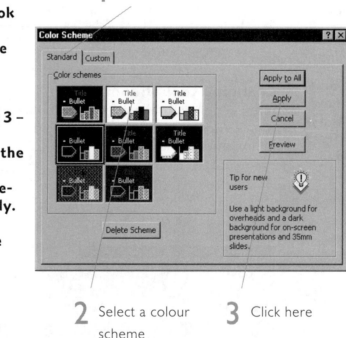

 Re step 3 – this applies the colour scheme to the pre-selected slide only. If you want to apply it to all the slides, click this button instead:

2 Select a colour scheme

3 Click here

Format Painter

PowerPoint 2000 offers a useful shortcut (the Format Painter) which enables you to copy a colour scheme:

- from one slide to another

- from one slide to multiple slides

If the Standard toolbar isn't currently on-screen, pull down the View menu and click Toolbars, Standard.

Copying colour schemes

In Slide Sorter view, select the slide whose colour scheme you want to transfer. Refer to the Standard toolbar; carry out step 1 for a single copy, or step 2 for multiple copies:

1 Click here

2 Double-click here

Re step 4 – if you followed step 1, click one slide. If you carried out step 2, click more than one.

3 Click the slide whose colour scheme you want to copy

If you followed step 2, press Esc when you've finished copying the colour scheme.

4 Click the slide(s) you want to apply the colour scheme to

Moving through presentations

You can broadcast slide shows over Intranets (with Internet Explorer 4 or later).
Pull down the Slide Show menu and click Online Broadcast, Set Up and Schedule. Click Set up and schedule a new broadcast, then OK. Complete the new dialog. Click Schedule Broadcast.

Since presentations – by their very nature – always have more than one slide, it's essential to be able to move from slide to slide easily (it's even more essential in the case of especially large presentations). There are two main methods you can use to do this.

Using the vertical scroll bar

In Normal or Notes Page views, move the mouse pointer over the vertical scroll box. Hold down the left mouse button and drag the box up or down. As you do so, PowerPoint 2000 displays a message box giving you the number and title of the slide you're up to.

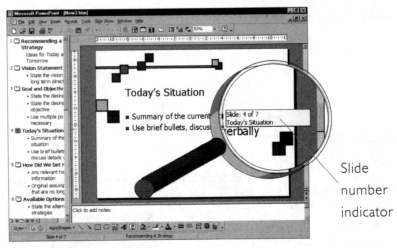

Slide number indicator

To start a broadcast, pull down the Slide Show menu and click Online Broadcast, Begin Broadcast. Click Start.

When the correct number displays, release the mouse button to jump to that slide.

Using Slide Sorter view

Slide Sorter view offers a useful shortcut which you can use to jump immediately to a specific slide. Simply double-click any slide icon within Slide Sorter view; PowerPoint 2000 then switches to Slide view and displays the slide you selected.

For help with any aspect of slide show broadcasting (inc. scheduling the broadcast via Outlook), see your system administrator.

Inserting and deleting slides

You can easily include existing slides from another slide show.

In Normal view, go to the slide after which you want the new slides inserted. Pull down the Insert menu and click Slides from Files. In the File field in the Slide Finder dialog, type in the address and file name of the second slide show. Click Display. In the Select slides section, click the slide(s) you want to include. Finally, click Insert.

You'll often want to insert a slide into presentation. There are also occasions when you'll need to delete a slide because it's no longer required. PowerPoint 2000 lets you do both easily and conveniently.

Inserting a slide

In Normal or Notes Page views, move to the slide that you want to precede the new one. In Slide Sorter view, click the relevant slide. Then pull down the Insert menu and click New Slide.

Now do the following:

The current slide format is highlighted; click another if you want to apply a new format

2 Click here

When you delete a slide, the slide and its contents are erased immediately, with no preliminary warning.

Deleting a slide

In Normal or Notes Page views, move to the slide that you want to delete. In Slide Sorter view, click a slide (or hold down Ctrl as you click multiple slide icons to delete more than one slide). Then pull down the Edit menu and click Delete Slide.

Inserting pictures

 To have a picture appear on every slide, insert it into the slide master (a template which applies to the overall slide show).

Pull down the View menu and click Master, Slide Master. Now launch the Clip Gallery or the Insert Picture dialog (see page 165) and insert a picture. To return to the active slide, do the following:

You can insert pictures into slide shows in two ways:

- with the Office Clip Gallery

- using a separate dialog

Inserting pictures via the Clip Gallery

In Normal or Notes Page views, go to the slide into which you want the clip art added. Pull down the Insert menu and click Picture, Clip Art. Now carry out the following steps:

Ensure this tab is activated

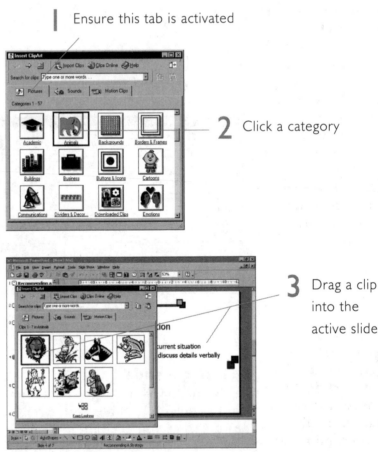

2 Click a category

Click here

 You can also use the Clip Gallery to insert movie and sound clips into slides. Simply activate the Sounds or Motion Clips tabs, select a category/clip then follow steps 3–4.

3 Drag a clip into the active slide

4 Release the mouse button – PowerPoint 2000 inserts the picture

Inserting pictures – the dialog route

In Normal or Notes Page views, go to the slide into which you want the picture added. Pull down the Insert menu and do the following:

Once inserted into a slide show, pictures can be resized and moved in the normal way – see pages 89–92 for guidelines.

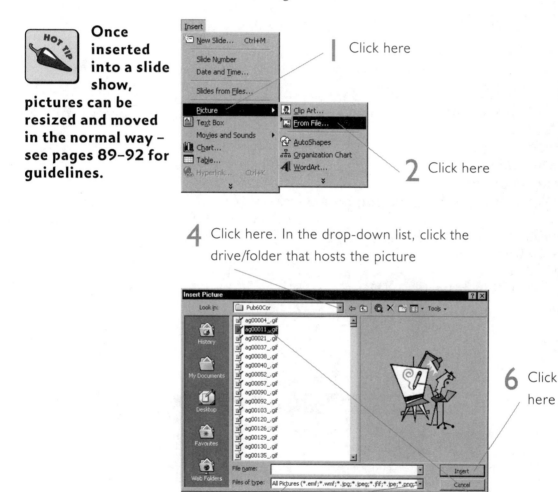

Click here

2 Click here

4 Click here. In the drop-down list, click the drive/folder that hosts the picture

6 Click here

3 Make sure All Pictures... is showing. If it isn't, click the arrow and select it from the drop-down list

5 Click a picture file

Inserting hyperlinks

You can insert hyperlinks into slides. In PowerPoint 2000, hyperlinks are 'action buttons' which you can click (while a presentation is being run) to jump to a prearranged destination immediately. This can be:

- preset slide targets (for instance, the first, last, next or previous slide)

- a specific slide (where *you* select a slide from a special dialog)

- a URL (providing you have a live Internet connection)

- another PowerPoint presentation

- another file

'URL' stands for Uniform Resource Locator. URLs are unique addresses for World Wide Web sites.
(For more information on the Internet, see 'Internet UK in easy steps'.)

Inserting an action button

In Normal or Notes Page view, pull down the Slide Show menu. Do the following:

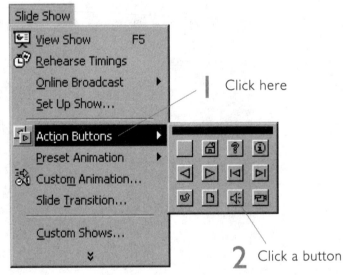

Now position the mouse pointer at the location on the slide where you want the button inserted. Hold down the left mouse button and drag to define the button. Release the mouse button and carry out the following steps:

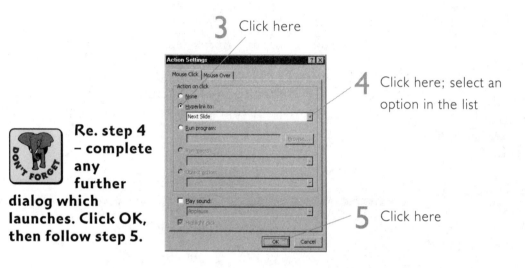

3 Click here

4 Click here; select an option in the list

5 Click here

 Re. step 4 – complete any further dialog which launches. Click OK, then follow step 5.

The illustration below shows an inserted action button/ hyperlink:

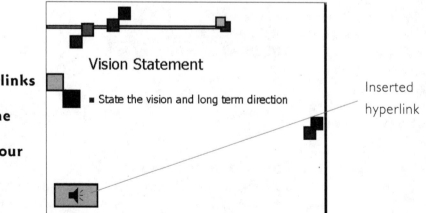

Vision Statement

■ State the vision and long term direction

Inserted hyperlink

Hyperlinks only become active when you run your slide show.

Printing

You can print any presentation component. These include:

- slides
- speaker notes
- outlines

Re step 4 – separate non-adjacent slides with commas but no spaces – e.g. to print slides 2, 5, 7 and 9 type in: 2,5,7,9

Enter contiguous slides with dashes – e.g. to print slides 2 to 7 inclusive, type in: 2-7

PowerPoint 2000 makes printing easy.

Printing a presentation

Pull down the File menu and click Print. Now carry out any of steps 1–5 below, as appropriate. Finally, follow step 6.

1 | Click here; select the printer you want from the list

2 Click here to print the current slide only

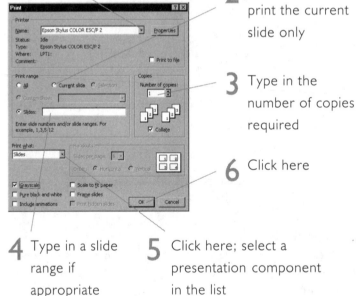

3 Type in the number of copies required

6 Click here

Ensure 'Grayscale' and 'Pure black and white' are deselected if you have a colour printer and want to print out in colour.

4 Type in a slide range if appropriate

5 Click here; select a presentation component in the list

Fast-track printing

To print using all the default settings, without launching the Print dialog, simply click this button on the Standard toolbar:

Running a presentation

Once you've created (and possibly printed) your slide show, it's time to run it. Before you do so, however, you should set the run parameters.

When you run your presentation you can, if you want, have PowerPoint 2000 wait for your command before moving from slide to slide. This is useful if you anticipate being interrupted during the presentation. You retain full control over delivery.

If you export slide shows to HTML format (see pages 171–172), you can view and run them in Internet Explorer.

Alternatively, you can have the slide show run automatically. Before you can do this, though, you have to set various parameters. These include the intervals between slides, which slides you want to run and the presentation type.

Preparing to run your slide show

First, open the presentation you want to run. Then pull down the Slide Show menu and click Set Up Show. Now do the following:

You can choose from a wide variety of slide show types:
  The first option – presentation by a speaker – is the most common.

If you don't want all the slides to run, enter start and end slide numbers

Re step 2 – click the following option:
Using timings, if present **to have the presentation run automatically.**

2 Select this if you want to control the slide show progression manually

3 Click here

Running a manual presentation

Pull down the Slide Show menu and click View Show. If you selected Manually in step 2 on page 169, PowerPoint 2000 runs the first slide of your presentation and pauses. When you're ready to move on to the next slide, left-click once or press Page Down. If you need to go back to the previous slide, simply press Page Up as often as required.

Rehearsing an automatic presentation

Before you can run an automatic presentation, you have to set the slide intervals. You can do this by 'rehearsing' the slide show. Pull down the Slide Show menu and click Rehearse Timings, then do the following:

This timer counts the interval until the next slide; when the timing is right, follow step 1

Click here

After step 1, PowerPoint 2000 moves to the next slide. Repeat step 1 until all the slides have had appropriate intervals allocated. Finally, do the following:

2 Click here

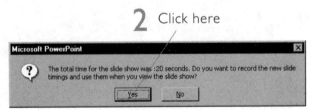

Running an automatic presentation

After rehearsal, pull down the Slide Show menu and click View Show. If you clicked 'Using timings, if present' in step 2 on page 169, PowerPoint 2000 displays the first slide and moves on to subsequent slides after the rehearsed intervals have elapsed.

Running presentations in Explorer

B. means that slide shows converted to HTML format and saved to the Web can be run by the majority of Internet users.

To convert a slide show to HTML, follow steps 1–4 on page 20. In step 1, however, select: Web Page (*.htm; *html)

You can hide the slide outline, if you want. Simply click here: (Repeat to unhide it.)

Here, the slide show is being displayed in Internet Explorer 5.

One corollary of Microsoft's elevation of the HTML format to a status which rivals that of its own formats is that:

A. presentations display authentically in Internet Explorer (especially if you're using version 4 or above)

B. you can even run presentations from within Internet Explorer

Running slide shows in Internet Explorer

First, use the techniques discussed on pages 21–22 to convert an existing presentation to HTML format. Open this in Internet Explorer. Now do the following:

Click here to run your show in Full-Screen mode

Internet Explorer now launches the first slide of your presentation so that it occupies the whole screen:

 For further coverage of essential PowerPoint 2000 features, see 'PowerPoint 2000', also in the 'in easy steps' series.

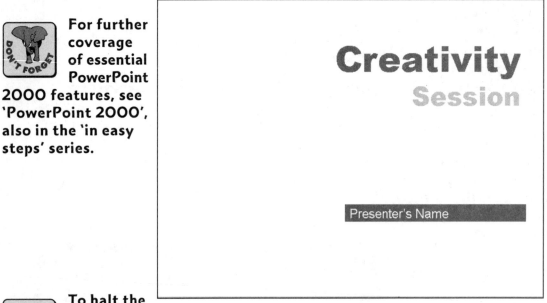

Creativity
Session

Presenter's Name

 To halt the slide show before the end, press

Esc.

Whether or not you selected 'Using timings, if present' in step 2 on page 169, Internet Explorer progresses to the next slide when the relevant interval has elapsed. And so on to the end...

When the last slide has been displayed, a special screen displays with the following text:

End of slide show, click to exit.

 To close Internet Explorer, press

Alt+F4.

Click anywhere to return to Internet Explorer's main screen.

Chapter Five

Outlook 2000

This chapter provides an introduction to the *stand-alone* (i.e. non-workgroup) use of Outlook 2000. You'll use the Outlook bar to launch any of Outlook's associated folders, then enter appointments/events, tasks and contact details; Outlook 2000 will then coordinate them so that you can manage your business/personal affairs more easily. You'll also use Outlook 2000 to compose, transmit, receive and reply to e-mail, using (optimally) Word 2000 as your editor. Finally, you'll surf the Internet directly from within Outlook 2000.

Covers

The Outlook 2000 screen

The Folder banner tells you which Outlook folder (in this case, Inbox) is active.

Below is a detailed illustration of a typical Outlook 2000 screen.

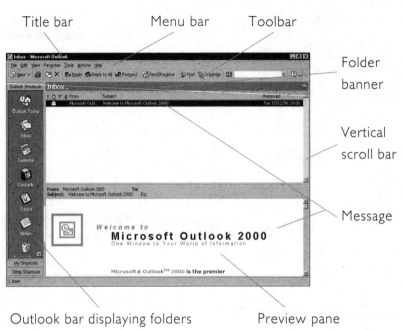

Title bar   Menu bar   Toolbar

Folder banner

Vertical scroll bar

Message

Outlook bar displaying folders   Preview pane

To print out work you do in any component on the Outlook bar, first click the relevant folder. Press Ctrl+P. Complete the Print dialog as normal. In particular, select a print style – the choices vary with the folder selected. (For more help with completing the Print dialog, see the relevant topic in earlier chapters in this book.)
Finally, click OK to begin printing.

Some of these – e.g. the Menu and scroll bars – are standard to just about all Windows programs. However, you can specify which of the four available toolbars display.

Specifying which toolbars display

Pull down the View menu and do the following:

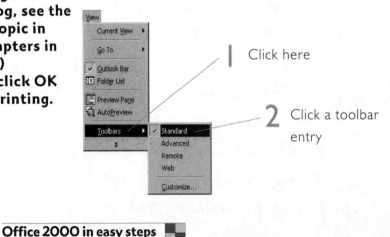

Click here

2 Click a toolbar entry

Using the Outlook bar

 Outlook 2000 organises its features into folders. All folders are accessible from the Outlook bar.

When you run Outlook 2000, it automatically opens the Inbox. This is the Outlook folder in which incoming messages are stored. However, there are several additional folders you can access. These include:

Calendar	A tool to help you schedule events, tasks, appointments and meetings
Contacts	A tool to help you manage business/personal contacts
Tasks	A task management aid
Notes	Acts as a jotting pad; you can create 'sticky' notes
Outbox	Messages waiting to be sent are stored here
Deleted Items	Self-explanatory

 To insert a note, click the Notes folder in the Outlook bar. Press Ctrl+N. Do the following:

Type in your note, then press Alt+F4.

Activating folders
Do the following:

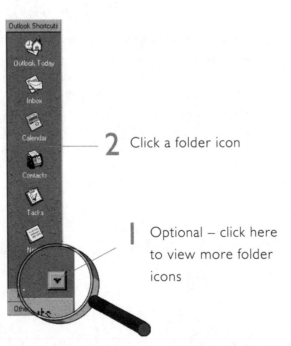

2 Click a folder icon

Optional – click here to view more folder icons

 To access additional delivery-based features, click here

My Shortcuts

 To access Windows folders, click here:

Other Shortcuts

The Calendar – an overview

Work Week view stresses the five days of the working week.

The Calendar provides alternative ways of viewing and interacting with your schedules. The main views are:

Day/Week/Month	The all-purpose view. An aspect of the Appointment Book; used to enter appointments, events and tasks. You can specify whether you work in the Day, Work Week, Week or Month aspects. (See below)
Active Appointments	An aspect of the Appointment Book; used to enter and monitor active appointments
Events	An aspect of the Appointment Book, useful for entering and monitoring events

If you want to switch to Events or Active Appointments views, pull down the View menu and click:

- Current View, Events, or;

- Current View, Active Appointments

respectively.

Some aspects of Outlook 2000 – for instance, the use of the Calendar to coordinate meetings among workgroup members – are beyond the scope of this book.

Switching between the Day, Work Week, Week and Month Calendars

You'll probably use Day/Week/Month view more than any other, because it offers great flexibility. By default, this view displays appointments etc. with the use of the Day aspect. To change the aspect, refer to the Standard toolbar and click any of the following:

The Outlook Today folder in the Outlook bar provides a handy summary of these areas:

- Mail
- Tasks
- Appointments

Week format

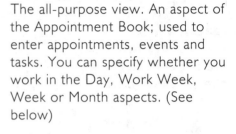

Day format

Work Week format

Month format

Using the Day Calendar

You can add appointments to the Day Calendar.

If you want, you can stipulate that the appointment is recurring (i.e. it's automatically entered at an interval you specify).

Re step 2 – if the date shown in the Date Navigator isn't correct, click:

◀ or ▶

to go back or forward by one month respectively.

If you need to mark a meeting as recurring, carry out steps 1–3. Then double-click the appointment in the Appointment Book. In the toolbar within the dialog which launches, click this button:

🔄 Recurrence...

In the Appointment Recurrence dialog, set the relevant options. Click OK. Now click the following:

💾 Save and Close

Adding an appointment in the Day Calendar

Carry out steps 1, 2 and 3 below (then follow the procedures in the DON'T FORGET tip if you want to mark the appointment as recurring):

2 Click the correct day

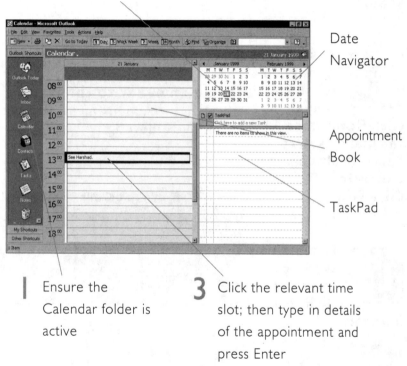

Date Navigator

Appointment Book

TaskPad

1 Ensure the Calendar folder is active

3 Click the relevant time slot; then type in details of the appointment and press Enter

Outlook adds the new appointment to the Calendar.

...cont'd

If you need to amend or update an existing event, double-click its button within the Appointment Book:

John's Birthday (Littlehampton)

Now follow steps 1–3 here, as appropriate.

Re step 1 – to mark an event as annual, click Recurrence. In the dialog, select Yearly (and complete any further fields). Click OK.

To mark an event as recurring, click this button:

Recurrence...

after steps 1–2. In the dialog which launches, set the relevant options. Click OK. Now perform step 3.

You can add events to the Daily Calendar.

Outlook 2000 handles events in a rather different way to appointments. For example, they don't occupy specific time slots in your Appointment Book. Instead, they can relate to any day and can even extend over more than one.

Outlook 2000 distinguishes between events and annual events. Annual events occur yearly on a specific date.

Examples of events include:

- birthdays and anniversaries

- shows

- seminars

Events display as buttons within the Appointment Book.

Adding an event to the Day Calendar

Pull down the Actions menu and click New All Day Event. Now do the following:

3 Click here   2 Enter a description

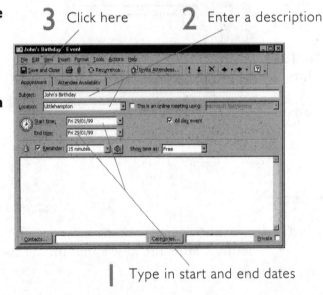

Type in start and end dates

Using the Week Calendars

You have to use a slightly different procedure to add appointments. Press Ctrl+N. Complete the dialog which launches in line with steps 1–3 on page 177, but also set Start and End times by completing these:

08:00

08:30

Use the Work Week or Week views as an alternative way to display your appointments and events.

In the Week Calendars, you can enter events and appointments. Enter events using the same procedures as for Day view. For appointments, see the HOT TIP.

Moving around in the Week Calendars

Pull down the View menu and click Go To, Go to Date. Carry out steps 1–4 and 7 to jump to a specific date in the Week Calendars, OR steps 5–7 as an alternative way to switch between views:

1 Click here

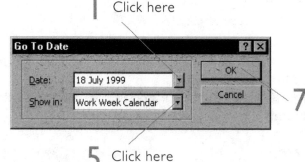

7 Click here

5 Click here

For further coverage of essential Outlook 2000 features, see 'Outlook 2000', also in the 'in easy steps' series.

2 Optional – click here to move 1 month back

3 Optional – click here to move 1 month forward

4 Click the day you want to view

6 Select a Calendar view

| Day Calendar |
| Week Calendar |
| Month Calendar |
| Work Week Calendar |

Using the Month Calendar

 You can use the Find tool in folders to locate specific data.

Pull down the Tools menu and click Find. Do the following:

A Enter search data

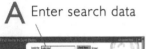

B Click here

(Ensure Search all text in... is selected for a more thorough search.)

Any matches are shown below the Find window.

To close Find, click this button:

Use the Month Calendar to gain a useful overview of your schedule.

Inserting a new appointment in the Month Calendar

Pull down the Actions menu and do the following:

| Click here

4 Click here   **3** Enter a description

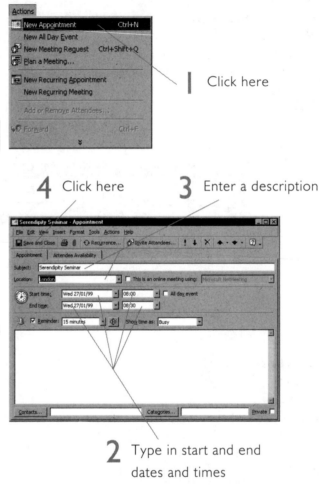

2 Type in start and end dates and times

 Click Reminder (then insert a reminder interval in the field to the right) if you want Outlook 2000 to prompt you when an appointment is due.

Inserting a new event in the Monthly Calendar

You can insert events in the Monthly Calendar by using the same techniques as for the Daily Calendar. Carry out steps 1–3 on page 178.

Working with the Tasks folder

Use the Tasks folder to enter and track tasks.

When you've entered a task into the Tasks folder, it displays in the TaskPad in the Daily, Work Week and Week Calendars.

If you need to amend or update an existing task, click within it and follow steps 1 and 2.

Entering a task

If the Tasks folder isn't already active, click the Tasks icon in the Outlook bar. Then do the following:

2 Type in a due date, then press Enter

Various views are available in the Tasks folder (the view shown here is Simple List**).**

   To switch between views, click Current View in the View menu; select a view in the sub-menu.

Click here; type in a task description

Tasks can be prioritised (Outlook recognises three levels: Low, Normal and High).

   To set a priority, click the Priority field and select one in the list.

Customising tasks

The above steps produce a basic task. If you want to customise the settings in more depth (for instance, you can set start and end dates, reminder intervals and/or priority levels), double-click the task after step 2. Complete the dialog which launches, then click Save and Close.

Working with the Contacts folder

Another view – Detailed Address Cards – uses the card model but with even more detail...

To switch between views, click Current View in the View menu; select a view in the sub-menu.

If you need to amend a contact, double-click it. Then carry out steps 3–4 as appropriate.

Use the Contacts folder as a convenient place to keep track of business/personal contacts.

Outlook displays contacts in various forms. The two main aspects are:

- as a grid

- using a business card model

You can enter contacts directly into either, but you may find that the business card view makes the job easier.

Entering a contact

If the Contacts view isn't already active, click the Contacts icon in the Outlook bar. Then do the following:

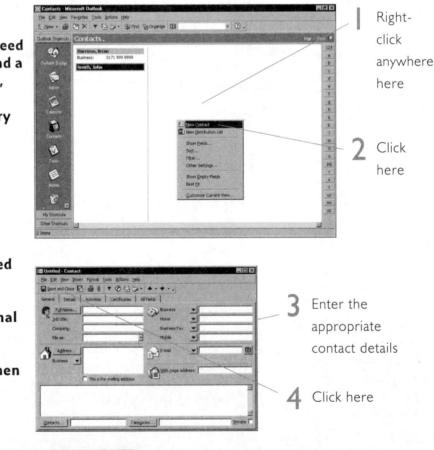

1 Right-click anywhere here

2 Click here

3 Enter the appropriate contact details

4 Click here

To set advanced contact details, click the additional dialog tabs. Complete the relevant fields then carry out step 4.

Composing e-mail

This book assumes you're using the Internet only method exclusively.
If you're using the second method, consult your system administrator for assistance.

Mail which you've written but which hasn't yet been sent is lodged in the Outbox folder. Mail which *has* been despatched is lodged in the Sent Items folder.

You can use Word 2000 as your e-mail editor directly from within Outlook 2000.
To do this, follow the procedures in the DON'T FORGET tip on page 46. Now press Ctrl+N from within Outlook's Inbox. Follow steps 1–4.

When you first launch it, Outlook runs the Outlook 2000 Startup wizard. This specifies which e-mail service options you use. There are two main choices:

Internet only	e-mail is sent only via an Internet Service Provider
Corporate/Workgroup	e-mail is sent via Microsoft Mail, Microsoft Exchange, third-party e-mail services or via an Internet Service Provider

The Startup wizard customises Outlook 2000 in line with the above (and further) choices made. As a result, you should have no difficulty in carrying out the instructions given here and later.

Composing e-mail

If the Inbox isn't currently open, click the Inbox icon in the Outlook bar. Pull down the File menu and click New, Mail Message. Do the following:

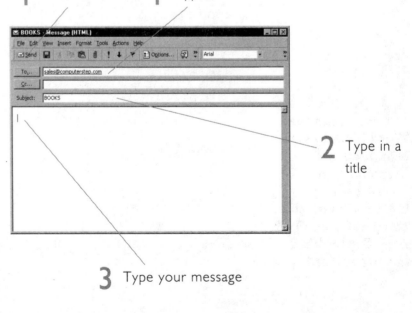

4 Click here

1 Type in the addressee

2 Type in a title

3 Type your message

Reading and replying to e-mail

 When you reply to e-mail, Outlook uses the format in which the original mail was sent.

 Re step 2 – to close the editor, press Alt+F4.

 This is the Preview pane: use it as a shortcut for viewing mail.

 Here, Outlook 2000 has launched Word 2000 as its e-mail editor. (Even if you haven't set up Outlook to do this, carry out steps 1–2 with Outlook's inbuilt editor.)

Reading e-mail

Once e-mail has been downloaded to you, you can read it in two ways. Do ONE of the following:

2 Double-click here; read the mail in the editor which launches

Read the mail here

Replying to e-mail

Carry out the following steps:

Click this button:  in the original message's overhead bar

3 Click here

2 Type in your reply

Sending/receiving e-mail

Before you can send/ receive e-mail, you may have to run a special wizard.

Pull down the Tools menu and click Remote Mail, Connect. Complete the wizard dialogs. These specify:

- which information service is used

- whether full messages are downloaded, or just informative headers

When the wizard is finished, Outlook logs on to your Service Provider.

The procedures here assume that you have Internet access. (For more information on Internet access and the Internet in general, see 'Internet UK in easy steps'.)

To send (and simultaneously receive) e-mail via an Internet Service Provider, do the following from within any of the e-mail related folders:

Click here

Outlook 2000 now establishes a connection to your Internet Service Provider and sends your e-mail. At the same time, it downloads any mail waiting for you:

When the process has finished, Outlook 2000 closes your Internet connection.

Surfing the Internet

Outlook 2000 has a special tool (Organize) which guides you through ways to customise features relating to the folder you're using – e.g. if you launch Organize over the Inbox, you're offered help in these areas:

• Using Folders
• Using Colors
• Using Views
• Junk E-Mail

From any of the major folders, pull down the Tools menu and click Organize. A special window launches. Do the following:

B Select and follow an action

A Click a topic

When you've finished, click this button:

You can:

• view Web pages directly from within Outlook 2000

• send Web pages as part of e-mail messages

Viewing Web pages

First, make sure your Internet connection is live. Refer to the Web toolbar (if isn't visible, click Toolbars, Web in the View menu) and do the following:

I Type in a Web address, then press Enter

The Web page displays

Sending Web pages

After you've carried out step 1 above (though not necessarily while you're still online), pull down the Actions menu and do the following:

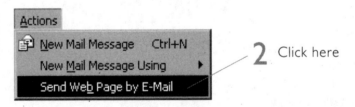

2 Click here

Outlook launches a new e-mail message with the Web page pre-loaded. Perform steps 1–4 on page 183. Then, if you went offline to carry out step 2 above, carry out the procedures on page 185 to send your Web page/message.

Index

F

Y